Walter Scott, James Arthur Tufts

Sir Walter Scott's

Lady of the Lake

Walter Scott, James Arthur Tufts

Sir Walter Scott's
Lady of the Lake

ISBN/EAN: 9783337119164

Printed in Europe, USA, Canada, Australia, Japan

Cover: Foto ©ninafisch / pixelio.de

More available books at **www.hansebooks.com**

Classics.

T'S
LADY OF THE LAKE.

ACADEMY

"... or prose either, it is a ... lors, and young people of ..."

COPYRIGHT, 1895,
BY LEACH, SHEWELL, & SANBORN.

ELECTROTYPED BY C. J. PETERS & SON.
PRESS OF BERWICK & SMITH.

PREFACE.

THE text of this edition follows closely that of the Edinburgh edition of 1821; but in a few places the reading of the *editio princeps* (1810) is given, both of which I found in the Harvard College Library.

The notes are such as I have found useful in my classes of various ages. Some of them will be unnecessary for the more advanced pupils; but all, I trust, will be found useful to one class or another.

I have defined the less common words for the sake of the younger pupils, who would hardly be expected to use a dictionary. The more advanced pupils, however, should be encouraged to use a dictionary, in order to find both the delicate shades of meaning, and also the etymology of many words.

I have tried to bring together in the Introduction interesting facts and opinions found in no other edition of this poem.

When *The Lady of the Lake* first appeared, Jeffrey said of it, in the *Edinburgh Review,* "We are of opinion that it will be oftener read hereafter than either of them [*The Lay of the Last Minstrel* and *Marmion*]. . . . It is more polished in its diction, and more regular in its versification; the story is constructed with infinitely more skill and address; there is a greater proportion of pleasing and tender passages, with much less antiquarian detail; and, upon the whole, a larger variety of characters, more artfully and judiciously contrasted. There is nothing so fine, perhaps, as the battle in *Marmion*, or so picturesque as some of the scattered sketches in the *Lay;* but there is a richness and a spirit in the whole piece which does not pervade either of those poems, — a profusion of incident and a shifting brilliancy of coloring that remind us of the witchery of Ariosto, and a constant elasticity and occasional energy which seem to belong more peculiarly to the author now before us."

Scott himself thought that the interest of *The Lay of the Last Minstrel* depended mainly upon the style, that of *Marmion* upon the descriptions, and that of *The Lady of the Lake* upon the incidents.

J. A. T.

THE PHILLIPS EXETER ACADEMY,
June, 1895.

BOOKS OF REFERENCE.

LOCKHART'S *Life of Sir Walter Scott.*
HUTTON'S *Life of Sir Walter Scott.* } *Encyclopædia Britannica.*
MINTO'S *Life of Sir Walter Scott.*
JEFFREY'S *Contributions to the Edinburgh Review.*
LESLIE STEPHEN'S *Hours in a Library* (First Series).
Essays by Carlyle, Hazlitt, Douglas Jerrold, and W. H. Prescott.
MRS. OLIPHANT'S *Literary History of England in the Eighteenth and Nineteenth Centuries.*
HUNNEWELL'S *Lands of Scott.*
HOWITT'S *Homes and Haunts of the British Poets.*
WASHINGTON IRVING'S *Visit to Abbotsford.*
C. R. LESLIE'S *Autobiographical Recollections.*
WORDSWORTH'S *Yarrow Revisited.*
RUSKIN'S *Modern Painters*, vol. iii.
BAGEHOT'S *Literary Studies*, vol. ii.
HOGG'S *Familiar Anecdotes.*
JERDAN'S *Men I Have Known.*
PHILLIPS'S *Popular Manual of English Literature.*
PANCOAST'S *Representative English Literature.*
PAINTER'S *Introduction to English Literature.*
PARSONS'S *English Versification.*

CONTENTS.

	PAGE
PREFACE	iii
BOOKS OF REFERENCE	v
INTRODUCTION	1
LIFE	1
PERSONAL APPEARANCE	3
DAILY HABITS	4
WRITINGS	4
SCOTT AS A POET	6
SCOTT AS A MAN	7
FRIENDS AND CONTEMPORARIES	9
THE LADY OF THE LAKE	13
NOTES	219

INTRODUCTION.

LIFE.[1]

WALTER SCOTT was born in Edinburgh, Aug. 15, 1771. His father, also named Walter, was an attorney of high rank, and his mother was Anne Rutherford, daughter of Dr. Rutherford, a distinguished professor and physician of Edinburgh. "My birth," says Scott, "was neither distinguished nor sordid. According to the prejudices of my country, it was esteemed *gentle*, as I was connected, though remotely, with ancient families both by my father's and mother's side. My father's grandfather was Walter Scott, well known by the name of *Beardie*. He was the second son of Walter Scott, first laird of Raeburn, who was third son of Sir Walter Scott, and the grandson of Walter Scott, commonly called in tradition *Auld Watt* of Harden. I am therefore lineally descended from that ancient chieftain, whose name I have made to ring in many a ditty, and from his fair dame, the Flower of Yarrow, — no bad genealogy for a Border Minstrel." — See LOCKHART'S *Life of Scott*, vol. i. ch. i.

He was the ninth child; the first six died very young.

"His father was conspicuous for methodical and thorough industry; his mother was a woman of imagination and culture. The son seems to have inherited the best qualities of the one, and acquired the best qualities of the other." — WM. MINTO, *Encyclopædia Britannica*.

[1] For full account see Books of Reference, p. 11.

Of delicate health, and lame from his second year, Scott spent much of his childhood in the country at Sandy Knowe. At the firesides of the country people, listening to old ballads and stories of Border warfare, he early acquired a taste for reading, and laid the foundations of his deep store of knowledge. In 1778 he entered the high school of Edinburgh, and remained about five years. He also had a private tutor. He entered the University of Edinburgh at the age of thirteen. In 1785, his health having somewhat improved, he decided on the profession of law. In 1792 he was admitted to the bar. He did not like his profession, however, and spent much of his time in indulging his antiquarian tastes. In 1797 he married Charlotte Margaret Carpenter, the daughter of a French Royalist, whose family, after the death of the father, had removed to England. They lived first at Edinburgh; and in 1798 he hired a cottage at Lasswade, where they lived till they removed to Ashestiel, in 1804. In 1799 he was made sheriff depute of Selkirkshire, with a salary of £300, and in 1806 a clerk of session. He received £1,600 a year from the two offices. This income, continued through twenty-five years, enabled him to make of literature "a staff and not a crutch." In 1811 he was able to purchase Abbotsford. In 1825 came the failure of Ballantyne and Company, publishers, with whom Scott was a partner. He gave up Abbotsford, and, refusing to take advantage of the bankrupt law, said to his creditors: "Gentlemen, time and I against any two. Let me take this good ally into company, and I believe I shall be able to pay you every farthing." From this time till his death he wrote with extraordinary rapidity. Ten novels in six years! In three years he earned for his creditors about £40,000; and if his health had not failed, probably he would have paid the whole debt. In 1830 he had a stroke of paralysis so severe that his physicians recommended a trip to Italy. In a frigate placed at his disposal by the government, he set sail for Naples in the autumn of 1831. He visited Rome, Venice, and other places of interest, and in the following April started home to die. He died at Abbotsford, Sept. 21, 1831.

PERSONAL APPEARANCE.

"When I last wrote I was about to be introduced to Sir Walter Scott. He quite answered all my expectations of him, and you may suppose they were very high. His manners are those of an amiable and unaffected man and a polished gentleman; and his conversation is something higher, for it is often quite as amusing and interesting as his novels, and without any apparent attempt at display. It flows from him in the most easy and natural manner. . . . He is tall and well-formed, excepting one of his ankles and foot (I think the right), which is crippled, and makes him walk very lamely. He is neither fat nor thin. His face is perfectly Scotch; and though some people think it heavy, it struck me as a very agreeable one. He never could have been handsome. His forehead is very high, his nose short, his upper lip long, and the lower part of his face fleshy. His complexion is fresh and clear, his eyes very blue, shrewd, and penetrating. I should say the predominant expression of his face is that of strong sense. His hair, which has always been very light (as well as his eyebrows and eyelashes), is now of a silvery whiteness, which makes him look somewhat older than he really is (I believe forty-six is his age)." — C. R. LESLIE: *Letter to Miss Leslie*, June 28, 1820.

"He was not quite forty-eight years old, tall and striking in his figure — full six feet in height, I think — stout and well-made. From the malconformation of one of his feet he stooped a little — at least that seemed to me the reason why he was somewhat prematurely bent; and his features bore the marks of coming age, which, like his gray hairs, had, I was told, much increased during the two preceding years. His countenance, as everybody knows, was dull when at rest; and even in common conversation, I think it expressed only much good nature and a remarkable willingness to listen. But his smile was uncommonly sweet and winning; and when he repeated poetry, which he loved to do, there was a transfiguration of his features which seemed to change their expression entirely. His deep, bluish-gray eyes, or rather the white portions of them, blushed and became pink with his emotion — an effect I have noticed in only a few other instances, and those in persons who possessed much sensibility." — GEORGE TICKNOR.

DAILY HABITS.

Lockhart tells us that at Ashestiel, Scott got up by five o'clock, worked at his desk till the family came to breakfast, between eight and nine, by which time he had done enough "to break the neck of the day's work." After breakfast he spent two hours more at his desk, and by noon was "his own man." "When the weather was too bad, he would labor incessantly all the morning; but the general rule was to be out and on horseback by one o'clock at the latest; while if any more distant excursion had been proposed over-night, he was ready to start on it by ten."

WRITINGS.

Scott began his literary career as a writer of ballads. He won considerable reputation by his translations from Bürger and Goethe, and by his Border Ballads. After the ballads

INTRODUCTION. 5

came *The Lay of the Last Minstrel,* in 1805; *Marmion,* in 1808; and *The Lady of the Lake,* the most popular of all, in 1810. Scott was paid two thousand guineas for *The Lady of the Lake. Waverley,* the first part of the Waverley Novels, appeared in 1814, followed by *Guy Mannering* in 1815, and others at the rate of nearly two each year. The last two, *Count Robert of Paris* and *Castle Dangerous,* did not appear till 1831, the year of Scott's death.

I. TRANSLATIONS, 1796–1800.

II. BALLADS.

Glenfinlas	1799	Cadyow Castle	1810
Eve of St. John	1799	English Minstrelsy	1810
The Grey Brothers	1799	The Battle of Sempach	1818
Border Minstrelsy	1802–1803	The Noble Moringer	1819

III. POEMS OF ROMANCE.

The Lay of the Last Minstrel	1805	Rokeby	1812
Marmion	1808	The Bridal of Triermain	1813
The Lady of the Lake	1810	The Lord of the Isles	1815
Vision of Don Roderick	1811		

IV. WAVERLEY NOVELS.

Waverley	1814	Peveril of the Peak	1823
Guy Mannering	1815	Quentin Durward	1823
The Antiquary	1816	St. Ronan's Well	1824
The Black Dwarf	1816	Redgauntlet	1824
Old Mortality	1816	The Betrothed	1825
Rob Roy	1818	The Talisman	1825
The Heart of Mid-Lothian	1818	Woodstock	1826
The Bride of Lammermoor	1819	The Two Drovers	1827
The Legend of Montrose	1819	The Highland Widow	1827
Ivanhoe	1820	The Surgeon's Daughter	1827
The Monastery	1820	The Fair Maid of Perth	1828
The Abbot	1820	Anne of Geierstein	1829
Kenilworth	1821	Count Robert of Paris	1831
The Pirate	1822	Castle Dangerous	1831
The Fortunes of Nigel	1822		

V. MISCELLANEOUS.

Reviews, Essays, Tales, Short Biographies, Memoirs, etc.

SCOTT AS A POET.

" The distinctive features of the poetry of Scott are ease, rapidity of movement, a spirited flow of narrative that holds our attention, an out-of-doors atmosphere and power of natural description, an occasional intrusion of a gentle personal sadness; and but little more. The subtle and mystical element, so characteristic of the poetry of Wordsworth and Coleridge, is not to be found in that of Scott, while in lyrical power he does not approach Shelley. We find instead an intense sense of reality in all his natural descriptions; it surrounds them with an indefinable atmosphere, because they are so transparently true. Scott's first impulse in the direction of poetry was given him from the study of the German ballads, especially Bürger's *Lenore*, of which he made a translation. As his ideas widened, he wished to do for Scottish Border life what Goethe had done for the ancient feudalism of the Rhine. He was at first undecided whether to choose prose or verse as his medium; but a legend was sent him by the Countess of Dalkeith, with a request that he would put it in ballad form. Having thus the framework for his purpose, he went to work, and *The Lay of the Last Minstrel* was the result. . . . The battle scene in *Marmion* has been called the most Homeric passage in modern literature; and his description of " The Battle of Beal' an Duine," from *The Lady of the Lake*, is an exquisite piece of narration, from the gleam of the spears in the thicket to the death of Roderick Dhu at its close. In the deepest sense, Scott is one with the spirit of his time in his grasp of fact, in that looking steadily at the object, which

Wordsworth had fought for in poetry, which Carlyle had advocated in philosophy. He is allied, too, to that broad sympathy for man which lay closest to the heart of the age's literary expression. Wordsworth's part is to inspire an interest in the lives of men and women about us; Scott's, to enlarge the bounds of our sympathy beyond the present, and to people the silent centuries. Shelley's inspiration is hope for the future; Scott's is reverence for the past." — PANCOAST'S *Representative English Literature.*

PROMINENT CHARACTERISTICS OF SCOTT AS A MAN.

Extraordinary Memory. — Mr. George Ticknor says that Scott repeated to him the English translations of two long Spanish ballads which he had never seen, but which had been read to him twice. Scott's college friend, John Irving, in writing of himself and Scott, says: "The number of books we thus devoured was very great. I forgot great part of what I read; but my friend, notwithstanding he read with such rapidity, remained, to my surprise, master of it all, and could even, weeks and months afterwards, repeat a whole page in which anything had particularly struck him at the moment."

Unsurpassed Conversational Powers. — "During the time of my visit," says Washington Irving, "he inclined to the comic rather than to the grave in his anecdotes and stories; and such, I was told, was his general inclination. He relished a joke or a trait of humor in social intercourse, and laughed with right good will. . . . His humor in conversation, as in his works, was genial, and free from all causticity. He had a quick perception of faults and foibles; but he looked upon human nature with an indulgent eye, relishing what was good and pleasant, tolerating what was frail, and pitying what was evil. . . . I do not recollect a sneer throughout his conversation, any more than there is throughout his works."

Sincerity and Honesty. — "I think," says Lord Byron, "that Scott is the only very successful genius that could be cited as being as generally beloved as a man as he is admired as an author; and, I must add, he deserves it; for he is so thoroughly good-natured, sincere, and honest, that he disarms the envy and jealousy his extraordinary genius must excite."

Uniform Courtesy and Hospitality. — "It would hardly, I believe," says Lockhart, " be too much to affirm that Sir Walter Scott entertained under his roof, in the course of the seven or eight brilliant seasons when his prosperity was at its height, as many persons of distinction in rank, in politics, in art, in literature, and in science, as the most princely nobleman of his age ever did in the like space of time."

Great Power of Mental Association. — "Scott, as all who saw him tell us," says Leslie Stephen, "could never see an old tower, or a bank, or a rush of a stream, without instantly recalling a boundless collection of appropriate anecdotes. He might be quoted as a case in point by those who would explain all poetical imagination by the power of associating ideas. He is the *poet of association.*"

Patriotism and Love of Family. — "The love of his country," says Lockhart, "became indeed a passion; no knight ever tilted for his mistress more willingly than he would have bled and died to preserve even the airiest surviving nothing of her antique pretensions for Scotland. But the Scotland of his affections had the clan Scott for her kernel."

High Veneration for Antiquity. — "His cranium, indeed," says Prescott, "to judge from his busts, must have exhibited a strong development of the organ of veneration. He regarded with reverence everything connected with antiquity."

Great Energy and Vigor. — "Yet, on the other hand," says Carlyle, "the surliest critic must allow that Scott was a genuine man, which itself is a great matter. No affectation, fantasticality, or distortion dwelt in him, no shadow of cant. Nay, withal, was he not a right brave and strong man according to his kind? What a load of toil, what a measure of felicity, he quietly bore along with him! with what quiet strength he both worked on this earth and enjoyed in it, invincible to evil fortune and to good!"

Extreme Fondness for Animals. — "But Scott's sympathies were not confined to his species," says Prescott; "and if he treated them like blood relations, he treated his brute followers like personal friends."

FRIENDS AND CONTEMPORARIES.

Among Scott's friends and contemporaries may be mentioned the following : —

John Irving, intimate friend in college.

Robert Burns, the poet, came to Edinburgh when Scott was fifteen years old.

James Ballantyne, the publisher.

James Hogg, the peasant poet, sometimes called the "Ettrick Shepherd."

Thomas Campbell, author of *Pleasures of Hope.*

William Wordsworth, the poet, a life-long friend.

Robert Southey, the poet, visited Scott at Ashestiel in 1805.

Joanna Baillie, the poet, visited Scott in 1808.

Lord Byron, the poet.

Sir Humphry Davy, the philosopher, a congenial friend and a visitor at Abbotsford.

Dugald Stewart, Archibald Alison, Sydney Smith, Lord

Brougham, Lord Jeffrey, William Clerk, Thomas Erskine, Sir William Hamilton, — all members of " The Friday Club."

Thomas Moore, the poet, a great admirer and a visitor at Abbotsford.

Goethe, the German poet.

Henry Hallam, the historian, visited Abbotsford in 1829.

Crabbe, the poet.

Maria Edgeworth, the novelist.

George Ticknor, the author.

Washington Irving visited Abbotsford in 1817.

John G. Lockhart, Scott's son-in-law and biographer.

THE LADY OF THE LAKE.

A POEM.

IN SIX CANTOS.

ARGUMENT.

The Scene of the following Poem is laid chiefly in the vicinity of Lock Katrine, in the Western Highlands of Perthshire. The time of Action includes Six Days, and the transactions of each Day occupy a Canto.

THE LADY OF THE LAKE.

CANTO FIRST.

The Chase.

HARP of the North! that moldering long hast hung
   On the witch-elm that shades Saint Fillan's spring,
And down the fitful breeze thy numbers flung,
   Till envious ivy did around thee cling,
Muffling with verdant ringlet every string, —
   O Minstrel Harp, still must thine accents sleep?
Mid rustling leaves and fountains murmuring,
   Still must thy sweeter sounds their silence keep,
Nor bid a warrior smile, nor teach a maid to weep?

Not thus, in ancient days of Caledon,   10
   Was thy voice mute amid the festal crowd,
When lay of hopeless love, or glory won,
   Aroused the fearful, or subdued the proud.
At each according pause, was heard aloud
   Thine ardent symphony sublime and high!

Fair dames and crested chiefs attention bow'd;
    For still the burden of thy minstrelsy
Was Knighthood's dauntless deed, and Beauty's matchless eye.

O wake once more! how rude soe'er the hand
    That ventures o'er thy magic maze to stray;   20
O wake once more! though scarce my skill command
    Some feeble echoing of thine earlier lay:
Though harsh and faint, and soon to die away,
    And all unworthy of thy nobler strain,
Yet if one heart throb higher at its sway,
    The wizard note has not been touch'd in vain.
Then silent be no more! Enchantress, wake again!

I.

    The stag at eve had drunk his fill,
    Where danced the moon on Monan's rill,
    And deep his midnight lair had made   30
    In lone Glenartney's hazel shade;
    But, when the sun his beacon red
    Had kindled on Benvoirlich's head,
    The deep-mouth'd bloodhound's heavy bay
    Resounded up the rocky way,
    And faint, from farther distance borne,
    Were heard the clanging hoof and horn.

THE CHASE.

II.

As Chief, who hears his warder call,
"To arms! the foemen storm the wall,"
The antler'd monarch of the waste   40
Sprung from his heathery couch in haste.
But, ere his fleet career he took,
The dew-drops from his flanks he shook;
Like crested leader proud and high,
Toss'd his beam'd frontlet to the sky;
A moment gazed adown the dale,
A moment snuff'd the tainted gale,
A moment listen'd to the cry,
That thicken'd as the chase drew nigh;
Then, as the headmost foes appear'd,   50
With one brave bound the copse he clear'd,
And, stretching forward free and far,
Sought the wild heaths of Uam-Var.

III.

Yell'd on the view the opening pack;
Rock, glen, and cavern, paid them back;
To many a mingled sound at once
The awaken'd mountain gave response.
An hundred dogs bay'd deep and strong,
Clatter'd a hundred steeds along,
Their peal the merry horns rung out,   60

An hundred voices join'd the shout;
With hark and whoop and wild halloo,
No rest Benvoirlich's echoes knew.
Far from the tumult fled the roe,
Close in her covert cower'd the doe,
The falcon, from her cairn on high,
Cast on the rout a wondering eye,
Till far beyond her piercing ken
The hurricane had swept the glen.
Faint, and more faint, its failing din   70
Return'd from cavern, cliff, and linn,
And silence settled, wide and still,
On the lone wood and mighty hill.

IV.

Less loud the sounds of sylvan war
Disturb'd the heights of Uam-Var,
And rous'd the cavern, where, 'tis told,
A giant made his den of old;
For ere that steep ascent was won,
High in his pathway hung the sun,
And many a gallant, stay'd perforce,   80
Was fain to breathe his faltering horse,
And of the trackers of the deer,
Scarce half the lessening pack was near;
So shrewdly on the mountain side,
Had the bold burst their mettle tried.

V.

The noble stag was pausing now
Upon the mountain's southern brow,
Where broad extended, far beneath,
The varied realms of fair Menteith.
With anxious eye he wander'd o'er 90
Mountain and meadow, moss and moor,
And ponder'd refuge from his toil,
By far Lochard or Aberfoyle.
But nearer was the copsewood gray
That waved and wept on Loch Achray,
And mingled with the pine-trees blue
On the bold cliffs of Benvenue.
Fresh vigor with the hope return'd,
With flying foot the heath he spurn'd,
Held westward with unwearied race, 100
And left behind the panting chase.

VI.

'Twere long to tell what steeds gave o'er,
As swept the hunt through Cambusmore;
What reins were tighten'd in despair,
When rose Benledi's ridge in air;
Who flagg'd upon Bochastle's heath,
Who shunn'd to stem the flooded Teith,
For twice that day, from shore to shore,
The gallant stag swam stoutly o'er.

Few were the stragglers following far, 110
That reach'd the lake of Vennachar;
And when the Brigg of Turk was won,
The headmost horseman rode alone.

VII.

Alone, but with unbated zeal,
That horseman plied the scourge and steel;
For jaded now, and spent with toil,
Emboss'd with foam, and dark with soil,
While every gasp with sobs he drew,
The laboring stag strain'd full in view.
Two dogs of black Saint Hubert's breed, 120
Unmatch'd for courage, breath, and speed,
Fast on his flying traces came,
And all but won that desperate game;
For, scarce a spear's length from his haunch,
Vindictive toil'd the bloodhound stanch;
Nor nearer might the dogs attain,
Nor farther might the quarry strain.
Thus up the margin of the lake,
Between the precipice and brake,
O'er stock and rock their race they take. 130

VIII.

The Hunter mark'd that mountain high,
The lone lake's western boundary,

THE CHASE.

And deem'd the stag must turn to bay,
Where that huge rampart barr'd the way;
Already glorying in the prize,
Measured his antlers with his eyes;
For the death-wound and death-halloo,
Muster'd his breath, his whinyard drew; —
But thundering as he came prepared,
With ready arm and weapon bared,   140
The wily quarry shunn'd the shock,
And turn'd him from the opposing rock;
Then, dashing down a darksome glen,
Soon lost to hound and Hunter's ken,
In the deep Trosachs' wildest nook
His solitary refuge took.
There, while close couch'd, the thicket shed
Cold dews and wild flowers on his head,
He heard the baffled dogs in vain
Rave through the hollow pass amain,   150
Chiding the rocks that yell'd again.

IX.

Close on the hounds the Hunter came,
To cheer them on the vanish'd game;
But, stumbling in the rugged dell,
The gallant horse exhausted fell.
The impatient rider strove in vain
To rouse him with the spur and rein,

For the good steed, his labors o'er,
Stretch'd his stiff limbs, to rise no more;
Then, touch'd with pity and remorse, 160
He sorrow'd o'er the expiring horse.
"I little thought, when first thy rein
I slack'd upon the banks of Seine,
That Highland eagle e'er should feed
On thy fleet limbs, my matchless steed!
Woe worth the chase, woe worth the day,
That costs thy life, my gallant gray!"

X.

Then through the dell his horn resounds,
From vain pursuit to call the hounds.
Back limp'd, with slow and crippled pace, 170
The sulky leaders of the chase;
Close to their master's side they press'd,
With drooping tail and humbled crest;
But still the dingle's hollow throat
Prolong'd the swelling bugle-note.
The owlets started from their dream,
The eagles answer'd with their scream,
Round and around the sounds were cast,
Till echo seem'd an answering blast;
And on the Hunter hied his way, 180
To join some comrades of the day;
Yet often paused, so strange the road,
So wondrous were the scenes it showed.

XI.

The western waves of ebbing day
Roll'd o'er the glen their level way;
Each purple peak, each flinty spire,
Was bathed in floods of living fire.
But not a setting beam could glow
Within the dark ravines below,
Where twined the path, in shadow hid,   190
Round many a rocky pyramid,
Shooting abruptly from the dell
Its thunder-splinter'd pinnacle;
Round many an insulated mass,
The native bulwarks of the pass,
Huge as the tower which builders vain
Presumptuous piled on Shinar's plain.
The rocky summits, split and rent,
Form'd turret, dome, or battlement,
Or seem'd fantastically set   200
With cupola or minaret,
Wild crests as pagod ever deck'd,
Or mosque of Eastern architect.
Nor were these earth-born castles bare,
Nor lack'd they many a banner fair;
For, from their shiver'd brows display'd,
Far o'er the unfathomable glade,
All twinkling with the dewdrop sheen,
The brier-rose fell in streamers green,

And creeping shrubs, of thousand dyes, 210
Waved in the west-wind's summer sighs.

XII.

Boon nature scatter'd, free and wild,
Each plant or flower, the mountain's child.
Here eglantine embalmed the air,
Hawthorn and hazel mingled there;
The primrose pale, and violet flower,
Found in each clift a narrow bower;
Fox-glove and night-shade, side by side,
Emblems of punishment and pride,
Group'd their dark hues with every stain 220
The weather-beaten crags retain.
With boughs that quak'd at every breath,
Gray birch and aspen wept beneath;
Aloft, the ash and warrior oak
Cast anchor in the rifted rock;
And, higher yet, the pine-tree hung
His shatter'd trunk, and frequent flung,
Where seem'd the cliffs to meet on high,
His boughs athwart the narrow'd sky.
Highest of all, where white peaks glanced, 230
Where glist'ning streamers waved and danced,
The wanderer's eye could barely view
The summer heaven's delicious blue;

So wondrous wild, the whole might seem
The scenery of a fairy dream.

XIII.

Onward, amid the copse 'gan peep
A narrow inlet, still and deep,
Affording scarce such breadth of brim
As served the wild duck's brood to swim.
Lost for a space, through thickets veering, 240
But broader when again appearing,
Tall rocks and tufted knolls their face
Could on the dark-blue mirror trace;
And farther as the Hunter stray'd,
Still broader sweep its channels made.
The shaggy mounds no longer stood,
Emerging from entangled wood,
But, wave-encircled, seem'd to float,
Like castle girdled with its moat;
Yet broader floods extending still 250
Divide them from their parent hill,
Till each, retiring, claims to be
An islet in an inland sea.

XIV.

And now, to issue from the glen,
No pathway meets the wanderer's ken,

Unless he climb, with footing nice,
A far projecting precipice.
The broom's tough roots his ladder made,
The hazel saplings lent their aid;
And thus an airy point he won, 260
Where, gleaming with the setting sun,
One burnish'd sheet of living gold,
Loch Katrine lay beneath him roll'd,
In all her length far winding lay,
With promontory, creek, and bay,
And islands that, empurpled bright,
Floated amid the livelier light,
And mountains, that like giants stand,
To sentinel enchanted land.
High on the south, huge Benvenue 270
Down to the lake in masses threw
Crags, knolls, and mounds, confusedly hurl'd,
The fragments of an earlier world;
A wildering forest feather'd o'er
His ruin'd sides and summit hoar,
While on the north, through middle air,
Ben-an heaved high his forehead bare.

XV.

From the steep promontory gazed
The stranger, raptured and amazed,
And, "What a scene were here," he cried, 280

"For princely pomp, or churchman's pride!
On this bold brow, a lordly tower;
In that soft vale, a lady's bower;
On yonder meadow, far away,
The turrets of a cloister gray;
How blithely might the bugle-horn
Chide, on the lake, the lingering morn!
How sweet, at eve, the lover's lute
Chime, when the groves were still and mute!
And, when the midnight moon should lave   290
Her forehead in the silver wave,
How solemn on the ear would come
The holy matin's distant hum,
While the deep peal's commanding tone
Should wake, in yonder islet lone,
A sainted hermit from his cell,
To drop a bead with every knell —
And bugle, lute, and bell, and all,
Should each bewilder'd stranger call
To friendly feast, and lighted hall.   300

XVI.

" Blithe were it then to wander here
But now, — beshrew yon nimble deer,
Like that same hermit's, thin and spare,
The copse must give my evening fare;
Some mossy bank my couch must be,

Some rustling oak my canopy.
Yet pass we that; the war and chase
Give little choice of resting-place; —
A summer night, in greenwood spent,
Were but to-morrow's merriment: 310
But hosts may in these wilds abound,
Such as are better miss'd than found;
To meet with Highland plunderers here
Were worse than loss of steed or deer. -
I am alone; — my bugle strain
May call some straggler of the train;
Or, fall the worst that may betide,
Ere now this falchion has been tried."

XVII.

But scarce again his horn he wound,
When lo! forth starting at the sound, 320
From underneath an aged oak,
That slanted from the islet rock,
A Damsel guider of its way,
A little skiff shot to the bay,
That round the promontory steep
Led its deep line in graceful sweep,
Eddying, in almost viewless wave,
The weeping willow twig to lave,
And kiss, with whispering sound and slow,
The beach of pebbles bright as snow. 330

The boat had touch'd this silver strand,
Just as the Hunter left his stand,
And stood conceal'd amid the brake,
To view this Lady of the Lake.
The maiden paused, as if again
She thought to catch the distant strain.
With head up-raised, and look intent,
And eye and ear attentive bent,
And locks flung back, and lips apart,
Like monument of Grecian art, 340
In listening mood, she seem'd to stand,
The guardian Naiad of the strand.

XVIII.

And ne'er did Grecian chisel trace
A Nymph, a Naiad, or a Grace,
Of finer form, or lovelier face!
What though the sun, with ardent frown,
Had slightly tinged her cheek with brown, —
The sportive toil, which, short and light,
Had dyed her glowing hue so bright,
Served too in hastier swell to show 350
Short glimpses of a breast of snow:
What though no rule of courtly grace
To measured mood had train'd her pace, —
A foot more light, a step more true,
Ne'er from the heath-flower dash'd the dew;

E'en the slight harebell raised its head,
Elastic from her airy tread:
What though upon her speech there hung
The accents of the mountain tongue,—
Those silver sounds, so soft, so dear,   360
The list'ner held his breath to hear!

XIX.

A chieftain's daughter seem'd the maid;
Her satin snood, her silken plaid,
Her golden brooch such birth betray'd.
And seldom was a snood amid
Such wild luxuriant ringlets hid,
Whose glossy black to shame might bring
The plumage of the raven's wing;
And seldom o'er a breast so fair,
Mantled a plaid with modest care,   370
And never brooch the folds combined
Above a heart more good and kind.
Her kindness and her worth to spy,
You need but gaze on Ellen's eye;
Not Katrine, in her mirror blue,
Gives back the shaggy banks more true,
Than every free-born glance confess'd
The guileless movements of her breast;
Whether joy danced in her dark eye,
Or woe or pity claim'd a sigh,   380

Or filial love was glowing there,
Or meek devotion pour'd a prayer,
Or tale of injury call'd forth
The indignant spirit of the North.
One only passion unreveal'd,
With maiden pride the maid conceal'd,
Yet not less purely felt the flame; —
O need I tell that passion's name!

XX.

Impatient of the silent horn,
Now on the gale her voice was borne: — 390
"Father!" she cried; the rocks around
Loved to prolong the gentle sound.
A while she paused, no answer came, —
"Malcolm, was thine the blast?" the name
Less resolutely utter'd fell,
The echoes could not catch the swell.
"A stranger I," the Huntsman said,
Advancing from the hazel shade.
The maid, alarm'd, with hasty oar,
Push'd her light shallop from the shore, 400
And when a space was gain'd between,
Closer she drew her bosom's screen;
(So forth the startled swan would swing,
So turn to prune his ruffled wing.)
Then safe, though flutter'd and amazed,

She paused, and on the stranger gazed.
Not his the form, nor his the eye,
That youthful maidens wont to fly.

XXI.

On his bold visage middle age
Had slightly press'd its signet sage, 410
Yet had not quench'd the open truth
And fiery vehemence of youth;
Forward and frolic glee was there,
The will to do, the soul to dare,
The sparkling glance, soon blown to fire,
Of hasty love, or headlong ire.
His limbs were cast in manly mould,
For hardy sport or contest bold;
And though in peaceful garb array'd,
And weaponless, except his blade, 420
His stately mien as well implied
A high-born heart, a martial pride,
As if a baron's crest he wore,
And sheath'd in armor trod the shore.
Slighting the petty need he show'd,
He told of his benighted road;
His ready speech flow'd fair and free,
In phrase of gentlest courtesy;
Yet seem'd that tone, and gesture bland,
Less used to sue than to command. 430

XXII.

A while the maid the stranger eyed,
And, reassured, at length replied,
That Highland halls were open still
To wilder'd wanderers of the hill.
"Nor think you unexpected come
To yon lone isle, our desert home;
Before the heath had lost the dew,
This morn, a couch was pull'd for you;
On yonder mountain's purple head
Have ptarmigan and heath-cock bled,   440
And our broad nets have swept the mere,
To furnish forth your evening cheer." —
"Now, by the rood, my lovely maid,
Your courtesy has err'd," he said;
"No right have I to claim, misplaced,
The welcome of expected guest.
A wanderer, here by fortune tost,
My way, my friends, my courser lost,
I ne'er before, believe me, fair,
Have ever drawn your mountain air,   450
Till on this lake's romantic strand,
I found a fay in fairy land."

XXIII.

"I well believe," the maid replied,
As her light skiff approach'd the side, —

"I well believe that ne'er before
Your foot has trod Loch Katrine's shore;
But yet, as far as yesternight,
Old Allan-bane foretold your plight, —
A gray-hair'd sire, whose eye intent
Was on the vision'd future bent. 460
He saw your steed, a dappled gray,
Lie dead beneath the birchen way;
Painted exact your form and mien,
Your hunting-suit of Lincoln green,
That tassell'd horn so gayly gilt,
That falchion's crooked blade and hilt,
That cap with heron plumage trim,
And you two hounds so dark and grim.
He bade that all should ready be,
To grace a guest of fair degree; 470
But light I held his prophecy,
And deem'd it was my father's horn,
Whose echoes o'er the lake were borne."

XXIV.

The stranger smiled: — "Since to your home
A destined errant-knight I come,
Announced by prophet sooth and old,
Doom'd, doubtless, for achievement bold,
I'll lightly front each high emprise,
For one kind glance of those bright eyes.

Permit me, first, the task to guide, 480
Your fairy frigate o'er the tide."
The maid, with smile suppress'd and sly,
The toil unwonted saw him try;
For seldom sure, if e'er before,
His noble hand had grasp'd an oar:
Yet with main strength his strokes he drew,
And o'er the lake the shallop flew;
With heads erect, and whimpering cry,
The hounds behind their passage ply.
Nor frequent does the bright oar break 490
The darkening mirror of the lake,
Until the rocky isle they reach,
And moor their shallop on the beach.

XXV.

The stranger view'd the shore around;
'Twas all so close with copsewood bound,
Nor track nor pathway might declare
That human foot frequented there,
Until the mountain-maiden show'd
A clambering unsuspected road,
That winded through the tangled screen, 500
And open'd on a narrow green,
Where weeping birch and willow round
With their long fibres swept the ground;

Here, for retreat in dangerous hour,
Some chief had framed a rustic bower.

XXVI.

It was a lodge of ample size,
But strange of structure and device;
Of such materials, as around
The workman's hand had readiest found.
Lopp'd of their boughs, their hoar trunks bared,
And by the hatchet rudely squared, 511
To give the walls their destined height,
The sturdy oak and ash unite;
While moss and clay and leaves combined
To fence each crevice from the wind.
The lighter pine-trees, overhead,
Their slender length for rafters spread,
And wither'd heath and rushes dry
Supplied a russet canopy.
Due westward, fronting to the green, 520
A rural portico was seen,
Aloft on native pillars borne,
Of mountain fir with bark unshorn,
Where Ellen's hand had taught to twine
The ivy and Idæan vine,
The clematis, the favor'd flower
Which boasts the name of virgin-bower,

And every hardy plant could bear
Loch Katrine's keen and searching air.
An instant in this porch she stayed,   530
And gayly to the stranger said,
"On heaven and on thy lady call,
And enter the enchanted hall!" —

XXVII.

"My hope, my heaven, my trust must be,
My gentle guide, in following thee." —
He cross'd the threshold — and a clang
Of angry steel that instant rang.
To his bold brow his spirit rush'd,
But soon for vain alarm he blush'd,
When on the floor he saw display'd,   540
Cause of the din, a naked blade
Dropp'd from the sheath, that careless flung
Upon a stag's huge antlers swung;
For all around, the walls to grace,
Hung trophies of the fight or chase:
A target there, a bugle here,
A battle-axe, a hunting spear,
And broadswords, bows, and arrows store,
With the tusk'd trophies of the boar.
Here grins the wolf as when he died,   550
And there the wild-cat's brindled hide

The frontlet of the elk adorns,
Or mantles o'er the bison's horns;
Pennons and flags defaced and stain'd,
That blackening streaks of blood retain'd,
And deer-skins, dappled, dun, and white,
With otter's fur and seal's unite,
In rude and uncouth tapestry all,
To garnish forth the sylvan hall.

XXVIII.

The wondering stranger round him gazed,   560
And next the fallen weapon raised; —
Few were the arms whose sinewy strength
Sufficed to stretch it forth at length.
And as the brand he poised and sway'd,
"I never knew but one," he said,
"Whose stalwart arm might brook to wield
A blade like this in battle-field."
She sigh'd, then smiled, and took the word;
"You see the guardian champion's sword:
As light it trembles in his hand,   570
As in my grasp a hazel wand;
My sire's tall form might grace the part
Of Ferragus or Ascabart;
But in the absent giant's hold
Are women now, and menials old."

XXIX.

The mistress of the mansion came,
Mature of age, a graceful dame;
Whose easy step and stately port
Had well become a princely court,
To whom, though more than kindred knew,   580
Young Ellen gave a mother's due.
Meet welcome to her guest she made,
And every courteous rite was paid,
That hospitality could claim,
Though all unask'd his birth and name.
Such then the reverence to a guest,
That fellest foe might join the feast
And from his deadliest foeman's door
Unquestion'd turn, the banquet o'er.
At length his rank the stranger names,   590
"The Knight of Snowdoun, James Fitz-James;
Lord of a barren heritage,
Which his brave sires, from age to age,
By their good swords had held with toil;
His sire had fall'n in such turmoil,
And he, God wot, was forced to stand
Oft for his right with blade in hand.
This morning, with Lord Moray's train
He chased a stalwart stag in vain,
Outstripp'd his comrades, miss'd the deer,   600
Lost his good steed, and wander'd here."

XXX.

Fain would the Knight in turn require
The name and state of Ellen's sire.
Well show'd the elder lady's mien,
That courts and cities she had seen;
Ellen, though more her looks display'd
The simple grace of sylvan maid,
In speech and gesture, form and face,
Show'd she was come of gentle race.
'Twere strange in ruder rank to find   610
Such looks, such manners, and such mind.
Each hint the Knight of Snowdoun gave,
Dame Margaret heard with silence grave;
Or Ellen, innocently gay,
Turn'd all inquiry light away:—
"Weird women we! by dale and down
We dwell, afar from tower and town.
We stem the flood, we ride the blast,
On wandering knights our spell we cast;
While viewless minstrels touch the string, 620
'Tis thus our charmed rhymes we sing."
She sung, and still a harp unseen
Fill'd up the symphony between.

XXXI.

Song.

"Soldier, rest! thy warfare o'er,
   Sleep the sleep that knows not breaking:
Dream of battled fields no more,
   Days of danger, nights of waking.
In our isle's enchanted hall,
   Hands unseen thy couch are strewing,
Fairy strains of music fall,   630
   Every sense in slumber dewing.
Soldier, rest! thy warfare o'er,
Dream of fighting-fields no more:
Sleep the sleep that knows not breaking,
Morn of toil, nor night of waking.

"No rude sound shall reach thine ear,
   Armor's clang or war-steed champing,
Trump nor pibroch summon here
   Mustering clan, or squadron tramping.
Yet the lark's shrill fife may come   640
   At the day-break from the fallow,
And the bittern sound his drum,
   Booming from the sedgy shallow.
Ruder sounds shall none be near,
Guards nor warders challenge here,
Here's no war-steed's neigh and champing,
Shouting clans or squadrons stamping."

XXXII.

She paused — then, blushing, led the lay
To grace the stranger of the day.
Her mellow notes awhile prolong
The cadence of the flowing song,
Till to her lips in measured frame
The minstrel verse spontaneous came.

Song Continued.

"Huntsman, rest! thy chase is done,
   While our slumbrous spells assail ye,
Dream not, with the rising sun,
   Bugles here shall sound reveillé.
Sleep! the deer is in his den;
   Sleep! thy hounds are by thee lying;
Sleep! nor dream in yonder glen,
   How thy gallant steed lay dying.
Huntsman, rest; thy chase is done,
Think not of the rising sun,
For at dawning to assail ye,
Here no bugles sound reveillé."

XXXIII.

The hall was clear'd — the stranger's bed
Was there of mountain heather spread,
Where oft an hundred guests had lain,
And dream'd their forest sports again.
But vainly did the heath-flower shed

Its moorland fragrance round his head;
Not Ellen's spell had lull'd to rest
The fever of his troubled breast.
In broken dreams the image rose
Of varied perils, pains, and woes:
His steed now flounders in the brake,
Now sinks his barge upon the lake;
Now leader of a broken host,
His standard falls, his honor's lost.
Then, — from my couch may heavenly might 680
Chase that worst phantom of the night! —
Again return'd the scenes of youth,
Of confident undoubting truth;
Again his soul he interchanged
With friends whose hearts were long estranged.
They come, in dim procession led,
The cold, the faithless, and the dead;
As warm each hand, each brow as gay,
As if they parted yesterday.
And doubt distracts him at the view — 690
O were his senses false or true!
Dream'd he of death, or broken vow,
Or is it all a vision now!

XXXIV.

At length, with Ellen in a grove
He seem'd to walk, and speak of love;

She listen'd with a blush and sigh,
His suit was warm, his hopes were high.
He sought her yielded hand to clasp,
And a cold gauntlet met his grasp:
The phantom's sex was changed and gone,   700
Upon its head a helmet shone;
Slowly enlarged to giant size,
With darken'd cheek and threatening eyes,
The grisly visage, stern and hoar,
To Ellen still a likeness bore. —
He woke, and, panting with affright,
Recall'd the vision of the night.
The hearth's decaying brands were red,
And deep and dusky lustre shed,
Half showing, half concealing, all   710
The uncouth trophies of the hall.
Mid those the stranger fix'd his eye
Where that huge falchion hung on high,
And thoughts on thoughts, a countless throng,
Rush'd, chasing countless thoughts along,
Until, the giddy whirl to cure,
He rose. and sought the moonshine pure.

XXXV.

The wild rose, eglantine, and broom,
Wasted around their rich perfume:

The birch-trees wept in fragrant balm, 720
The aspens slept beneath the calm;
The silver light, with quivering glance,
Play'd on the water's still expanse, —
Wild were the heart whose passions' sway
Could rage beneath the sober ray!
He felt its calm, that warrior guest,
While thus he communed with his breast: —
"Why is it, at each turn I trace
Some memory of that exiled race?
Can I not mountain-maiden spy, 730
But she must bear the Douglas eye?
Can I not view a Highland brand,
But it must match the Douglas hand?
Can I not frame a fever'd dream,
But still the Douglas is the theme? —
I'll dream no more — by manly mind
Not even in sleep is will resign'd.
My midnight orisons said o'er,
I'll turn to rest, and dream no more." —
His midnight orisons he told, 740
A prayer with every bead of gold,
Consign'd to heaven his cares and woes,
And sunk in undisturb'd repose;
Until the heath-cock shrilly crew,
And morning dawn'd on Benvenue.

CANTO SECOND.

The Island.

I.

At morn the black-cock trims his jetty wing,
   'Tis morning prompts the linnet's blithest lay,
All Nature's children feel the matin spring
   Of life reviving, with reviving day;
And while yon little bark glides down the bay,
   Wafting the stranger on his way again,
Morn's genial influence roused a minstrel gray,
   And sweetly o'er the lake was heard thy strain,
Mix'd with the sounding harp, O white-hair'd Allan-bane!

II.

Song.

"Not faster yonder rowers' might
   Flings from their oars the spray,
Not faster yonder rippling bright,
That tracks the shallop's course in light,
   Melts in the lake away,

Than men from memory erase
The benefits of former days;
Then, stranger, go! good speed the while,
Nor think again of the lonely isle.

"High place to thee in royal court,
   High place in battled line,   20
Good hawk and hound for sylvan sport,
Where beauty sees the brave resort,
   The honor'd meed be thine!
True be thy sword, thy friend sincere,
Thy lady constant, kind, and dear,
And lost in love's and friendship's smile
Be memory of the lonely isle.

III.

Song Continued.

"But if beneath yon southern sky
   A plaided stranger roam,
Whose drooping crest and stifled sigh,   30
And sunken cheek and heavy eye,
   Pine for his Highland home;
Then, warrior, then be thine to show
The care that soothes a wanderer's woe;
Remember then thy hap ere while,
A stranger in the lonely isle.

"Or if on life's uncertain main
    Mishap shall mar thy sail;
If faithful, wise, and brave in vain,
Woe, want, and exile thou sustain
    Beneath the fickle gale;
Waste not a sigh on fortune changed,
On thankless courts, or friends estranged,
But come where kindred worth shall smile,
To greet thee in the lonely isle."

IV.

As died the sounds upon the tide,
The shallop reach'd the mainlaind side,
And ere his onward way he took,
The stranger cast a lingering look,
Where easily his eye might reach
The Harper on the islet beach,
Reclined against a blighted tree,
As wasted, gray, and worn as he.
To minstrel meditation given,
His reverend brow was raised to heaven,
As from the rising sun to claim
A sparkle of inspiring flame.
His hand, reclined upon the wire,
Seem'd watching the awakening fire;
So still he sate, as those who wait
Till judgment speak the doom of fate;

So still, as if no breeze might dare
To lift one lock of hoary hair;
So still, as life itself were fled
In the last sound his harp had sped.

V.

Upon a rock with lichens wild,
Beside him Ellen sate and smiled. —
Smiled she to see the stately drake
Lead forth his fleet upon the lake,
While her vex'd spaniel, from the beach,   70
Bay'd at the prize beyond his reach?
Yet tell me, then, the maid who knows,
Why deepen'd on her cheek the rose? —
Forgive, forgive, Fidelity!
Perchance the maiden smiled to see
Yon parting lingerer wave adieu,
And stop and turn to wave anew;
And, lovely ladies, ere your ire
Condemn the heroine of my lyre,
Show me the fair would scorn to spy,   80
And prize such conquest of her eye!

VI.

While yet ne loiter'd on the spot,
It seem'd as Ellen mark'd him not;

But when he turn'd him to the glade,
One courteous parting sign she made;
And after, oft the knight would say,
That not when prize of festal day
Was dealt him by the brightest fair
Who e'er wore jewel in her hair,
So highly did his bosom swell,   90
As at that simple mute farewell.
Now with a trusty mountain-guide,
And his dark stag-hounds by his side,
He parts — the maid, unconscious still,
Watch'd him wind slowly round the hill;
But when his stately form was hid,
The guardian in her bosom chid. —
"Thy Malcolm! vain and selfish Maid!"
'Twas thus upbraiding conscience said,
"Not so had Malcolm idly hung   100
On the smooth phrase of southern tongue;
Not so had Malcolm strain'd his eye,
Another step than thine to spy. —
Wake, Allan-bane," aloud she cried,
To the old Minstrel by her side,
"Arouse thee from thy moody dream!
I'll give thy harp heroic theme,
And warm thee with a noble name;
Pour forth the glory of the Græme!" —
Scarce from her lip the word had rush'd,   110

When deep the conscious maiden blush'd;
For of his clan in hall and bower,
Young Malcolm Græme was held the flower.

VII.

The minstrel waked his harp — three times
Arose the well-known martial chimes,
And thrice their high heroic pride
In melancholy murmurs died.
"Vainly thou bid'st, O noble maid,"
Clasping his wither'd hands, he said,
— "Vainly thou bid'st me wake the strain,   120
Though all unwont to bid in vain.
Alas! than mine a mightier hand
Has tuned my harp, my strings has spann'd!
I touch the chords of joy, but low
And mournful answer notes of woe;
And the proud march, which victors tread,
Sinks in the wailing for the dead. —
O well for me, if mine alone
That dirge's deep prophetic tone!
If, as my tuneful fathers said,   130
This harp, which erst Saint Modan sway'd,
Can thus its master's fate foretell,
Then welcome be the minstrel's knell!

VIII.

"But ah! dear lady, thus it sigh'd,
The eve thy sainted mother died;
And such the sounds which, while I strove
To wake a lay of war or love,
Came marring all the festal mirth,
Appalling me who gave them birth,
And, disobedient to my call, 140
Wail'd loud through Bothwell's banner'd hall,
Ere Douglases, to ruin driven,
Were exiled from their native heaven. —
Oh! if yet worse mishap and woe,
My master's house must undergo,
Or ought but weal to Ellen fair,
Brood in these accents of despair,
No future bard, sad Harp! shall fling
Triumph or rapture from thy string;
One short, one final strain shall flow, 150
Fraught with unutterable woe,
Then shiver'd shall thy fragments lie,
Thy master cast him down and die!"

IX.

Soothing she answer'd him, — "Assuage,
Mine honor'd friend, the fears of age;
All melodies to thee are known,
That harp has rung or pipe has blown,

In Lowland vale or Highland glen,
From Tweed to Spey — what marvel, then,
At times, unbidden notes should rise, 160
Confusedly bound in memory's ties,
Entangling, as they rush along,
The war-march with the funeral song? —
Small ground is now for boding fear;
Obscure, but safe, we rest us here.
My sire, in native virtue great,
Resigning lordship, lands, and state,
Not then to fortune more resign'd,
Than yonder oak might give the wind;
The graceful foliage storms may reave, 170
The noble stem they cannot grieve.
For me," — she stoop'd, and, looking round,
Pluck'd a blue harebell from the ground, —
" For me, whose memory scarce conveys
An image of more splendid days,
This little flower, that loves the lea,
May well my simple emblem be;
It drinks heaven's dew as blithe as rose
That in the King's own garden grows;
And when I place it in my hair, 180
Allan, a bard is bound to swear
He ne'er saw coronet so fair." —
Then playfully the chaplet wild
She wreath'd in her dark locks, and smiled.

X.

Her smile, her speech, with winning sway,
Wiled the old harper's mood away.
With such a look as hermits throw
When angels stoop to soothe their woe,
He gazed, till fond regret and pride
Thrill'd to a tear, then thus replied : 190
" Loveliest and best ! thou little know'st
The rank, the honors, thou hast lost !
O might I live to see thee grace,
In Scotland's court, thy birth-right place,
To see my favorite's step advance,
The lightest in the courtly dance,
The cause of every gallant's sigh,
And leading star of every eye,
And theme of every minstrel's art,
The Lady of the Bleeding Heart ! " 200

XI.

" Fair dreams are these," the maiden cried,
(Light was her accent, yet she sigh'd,)
" Yet is this mossy rock to me
Worth splendid chair and canopy ;
Nor would my footsteps spring more gay
In courtly dance than blithe strathspey,
Nor half so pleased mine ear incline
To royal minstrel's lay as thine.

THE ISLAND.

And then for suitors proud and high,
To bend before my conquering eye, — 210
Thou, flattering bard! thyself wilt say,
That grim Sir Roderick owns its sway.
The Saxon scourge, Clan-Alpine's pride,
The terror of Loch Lomond's side,
Would, at my suit, thou know'st, delay
A Lennox foray — for a day." —

XII.

The ancient bard his glee repress'd;
" Ill hast thou chosen theme for jest!
For who, through all this western wild,
Named Black Sir Roderick e'er, and smiled! 220
In Holy-Rood a knight he slew;
I saw, when back the dirk he drew,
Courtiers give place before the stride
Of the undaunted homicide;
And since, though outlaw'd, hath his hand
Full sternly kept his mountain land.
Who else dared give, — ah! woe the day,
That I such hated truth should say —
The Douglas, like a stricken deer,
Disown'd by every noble peer, 230
Even the rude refuge we have here?
Alas, this wild marauding Chief
Alone might hazard our relief,

And now thy maiden charms expand,
Looks for his guerdon in thy hand;
Full soon may dispensation sought,
To back his suit, from Rome be brought.
Then, though an exile on the hill,
Thy father, as the Douglas, still
Be held in reverence and fear;   240
And though to Roderick thou'rt so dear
That thou might'st guide with silken thread,
Slave of thy will, this chieftain dread,
Yet, O loved maid, thy mirth refrain!
Thy hand is on a lion's mane." —

XIII.

"Minstrel," the maid replied, and high
Her father's soul glanced from her eye,
"My debts to Roderick's house I know;
All that a mother could bestow,
To Lady Margaret's care I owe,   250
Since first an orphan in the wild
She sorrowed o'er her sister's child;
To her brave chieftain son, from ire
Of Scotland's king who shrouds my sire,
A deeper, holier debt is owed;
And, could I pay it with my blood,
Allan! Sir Roderick should command

My blood, my life, — but not my hand.
Rather will Ellen Douglas dwell
A votaress in Maronnan's cell; 260
Rather through realms beyond the sea,
Seeking the world's cold charity,
Where ne'er was spoke a Scottish word,
And ne'er the name of Douglas heard,
An outcast pilgrim will she rove,
Than wed the man she cannot love.

XIV.

"Thou shakest, good friend, thy tresses gray —
That pleading look, what can it say
But what I own ? — I grant him brave,
But wild as Bracklinn's thundering wave; 270
And generous — save vindictive mood
Or jealous transport chafe his blood:
I grant him true to friendly band,
As his claymore is to his hand;
But O ! that very blade of steel
More mercy for a foe would feel:
I grant him liberal, to fling
Among his clan the wealth they bring,
When back by lake and glen they wind,
And in the Lowland leave behind, 280
Where once some pleasant hamlet stood,
A mass of ashes slaked with blood.

The hand that for my father fought,
I honor, as his daughter ought;
But can I clasp it reeking red,
From peasants slaughter'd in their shed?
No! wildly while his virtues gleam,
They make his passions darker seem,
And flash along his spirit high,
Like lightning o'er the midnight sky.   290
While yet a child, — and children know,
Instinctive taught, the friend and foe, —
I shudder'd at his brow of gloom,
His shadowy plaid, and sable plume;
A maiden grown, I ill could bear
His haughty mien and lordly air:
But, if thou join'st a suitor's claim,
In serious mood, to Roderick's name,
I thrill with anguish! or, if e'er
A Douglas knew the word, with fear.   300
To change such odious theme were best, —
What think'st thou of our stranger guest?" —

XV.

" What think I of him? — woe the while
That brought such wanderer to our isle!
Thy father's battle-brand, of yore
For Tine-man forged by fairy lore,
What time he leagued, no longer foes,

His Border spears with Hotspur's bows,
Did, self-unscabbarded, foreshow
The footstep of a secret foe.   310
If courtly spy hath harbor'd here,
What may we for the Douglas fear?
What for this island, deem'd of old
Clan-Alpine's last and surest hold?
If neither spy nor foe, I pray
What yet may jealous Roderick say?
— Nay, wave not thy disdainful head,
Bethink thee of the discord dread
That kindled when at Beltane game
Thou ledst the dance with Malcolm Græme;   320
Still, though thy sire the peace renew'd,
Smoulders in Roderick's breast the feud;
Beware! — But hark, what sounds are these?
My dull ears catch no faltering breeze,
No weeping birch, nor aspens wake,
Nor breath is dimpling in the lake,
Still is the canna's hoary beard,
Yet, by my minstrel faith, I heard —
And hark again! some pipe of war
Sends the bold pibroch from afar." —   330

XVI.

Far up the lengthen'd lake were spied
Four darkening specks upon the tide,

That, slow enlarging on the view,
Four mann'd and masted barges grew,
And, bearing downwards from Glengyle,
Steer'd full upon the lonely isle;
The point of Brianchoil they passed,
And, to the windward as they cast,
Against the sun they gave to shine
The bold Sir Roderick's banner'd Pine. 340
Nearer and nearer as they bear,
Spears, pikes, and axes flash in air.
Now might you see the tartans brave,
And plaids and plumage dance and wave:
Now see the bonnets sink and rise,
As his tough oar the rower plies;
See, flashing at each sturdy stroke,
The wave ascending into smoke;
See the proud pipers on the bow,
And mark the gaudy streamers flow 350
From their loud chanters down, and sweep
The furrow'd bosom of the deep,
As, rushing through the lake amain,
They plied the ancient Highland strain.

XVII.

Ever, as on they bore, more loud
And louder rung the pibroch proud.
At first the sound, by distance tame,

THE ISLAND. 59

Mellow'd along the waters came,
And, lingering long by cape and bay,
Wail'd every harsher note away, 360
Then bursting bolder on the ear,
The clan's shrill Gathering they could hear;
Those thrilling sounds, that call the might
Of Old Clan-Alpine to the fight.
Thick beat the rapid notes, as when
The mustering hundreds shake the glen,
And hurrying at the signal dread,
The batter'd earth returns their tread.
Then prelude light, of livelier tone,
Express'd their merry marching on, 370
Ere peal of closing battle rose,
With mingled outcry, shrieks, and blows;
And mimic din of stroke and ward,
As broadsword upon target jarr'd;
And groaning pause, ere yet again,
Condensed, the battle yell'd amain;
The rapid charge, the rallying shout,
Retreat borne headlong into rout,
And bursts of triumph, to declare
Clan-Alpine's conquest — all were there. 380
Nor ended thus the strain; but slow
Sunk in a moan prolong'd and low,
And changed the conquering clarion swell,
For wild lament o'er those that fell.

XVIII.

The war pipes ceased; but lake and hill
Were busy with their echoes still;
And, when they slept, a vocal strain
Bade their hoarse chorus wake again,
While loud a hundred clansmen raise
Their voices in their Chieftain's praise.   390
Each boatman, bending to his oar,
With measured sweep the burden bore,
In such wild cadence as the breeze
Makes through December's leafless trees.
The chorus first could Allan know,
"Roderich Vich Alpine, ho! iro!"
And near, and nearer as they row'd,
Distinct the martial ditty flow'd.

XIX.

Boat Song.

Hail to the chief who in triumph advances!
  Honor'd and bless'd be the ever-green Pine!   400
Long may the tree, in his banner that glances,
  Flourish, the shelter and grace of our line!
    Heaven send it happy dew,
    Earth lend it sap anew,
Gayly to bourgeon, and broadly to grow,
    While every Highland glen
    Sends our shout back agen,
"Roderich Vich Alpine dhu, ho! ieroe!"

Ours is no sapling, chance-sown by the fountain,
    Blooming at Beltane, in winter to fade;   410
When the whirlwind has stripp'd every leaf on the
        mountain,
    The more shall Clan-Alpine exult in her shade.
        Moor'd in the rifted rock,
        Proof to the tempest's shock,
Firmer he roots him the ruder it blow:
        Menteith and Breadalbane, then,
        Echo his praise agen,
" Roderich Vich Alpine dhu, ho! iereo!"

XX.

Proudly our pibroch has thrill'd in Glen Fruin,
    And Bannochar's groans to our slogan replied; 420
Glen Luss and Ross-dhu, they are smoking in ruin,
    And the best of Loch Lomond lie dead on her side.
        Widow and Saxon maid,
        Long shall lament our raid,
    Think of Clan-Alpine with fear and with woe;
        Lennox and Leven-glen
        Shake when they hear agen,
" Roderich Vich Alpine dhu, ho! ieroe!"

Row, vassals, row, for the pride of the Highlands!
    Stretch to your oars, for the ever-green Pine! 430
O that the rose-bud that graces yon islands,
    Were wreathed in a garland around him to twine!

O that some seedling gem,
Worthy such noble stem,
Honor'd and bless'd in their shadow might grow!
Loud should Clan-Alpine then
Ring from her deepmost glen,
"Roderich Vich Alpine dhu, ho! ieroe!"

XXI.

With all her joyful female band,
Had Lady Margaret sought the strand. 440
Loose on the breeze their tresses flew,
And high their snowy arms they threw,
As echoing back with shrill acclaim,
And chorus wild, the Chieftain's name;
While, prompt to please, with mother's art,
The darling passion of his heart,
The Dame called Ellen to the strand,
To greet her kinsman ere he land:
"Come, loiterer, come! a Douglas thou,
And shun to wreathe a victor's brow?" 450
Reluctantly and slow, the maid
The unwelcome summoning obey'd,
And, when a distant bugle rung,
In the mid-path aside she sprung: —
"List, Allan-bane! From mainland cast
I hear my father's signal blast.
Be ours," she cried, "the skiff to guide,

And waft him from the mountain-side." —
Then, like a sunbeam, swift and bright,
She darted to her shallop light, 460
And, eagerly while Roderick scann'd,
For her dear form, his mother's band,
The islet far behind her lay,
And she had landed in the bay.

XXII.

Some feelings are to mortals given,
With less of earth in them than heaven:
And if there be a human tear
From passion's dross refined and clear,
A tear so limpid and so meek,
It would not stain an angel's cheek, 470
'Tis that which pious fathers shed
Upon a duteous daughter's head!
And as the Douglas to his breast
His darling Ellen closely press'd,
Such holy drops her tresses steep'd,
Though 'twas an hero's eye that weep'd.
Nor while on Ellen's faltering tongue
Her filial welcomes crowded hung,
Mark'd she, that fear (affection's proof)
Still held a graceful youth aloof; 480
No! not till Douglas named his name,
Although the youth was Malcolm Græme.

XXIII.

Allan, with wistful look the while,
Mark'd Roderick landing on the isle;
His master piteously he eyed,
Then gazed upon the Chieftain's pride,
Then dash'd, with hasty hand, away
From his dimm'd eye the gathering spray;
And Douglas, as his hand he laid
On Malcolm's shoulder, kindly said,   490
"Canst thou, young friend, no meaning spy
In my poor follower's glistening eye?
I'll tell thee:— he recalls the day,
When in my praise he led the lay
O'er the arch'd gate of Bothwell proud,
While many a minstrel answer'd loud,
When Percy's Norman pennon, won
In bloody field, before me shone,
And twice ten knights, the least a name
As mighty as yon Chief may claim,   500
Gracing my pomp, behind me came.
Yet trust me, Malcolm, not so proud
Was I of all that marshall'd crowd,
Though the waned crescent own'd my might,
And in my train troop'd lord and knight,
Though Blantyre hymn'd her holiest lays,
And Bothwell's bards flung back my praise,
As when this old man's silent tear,

And this poor maid's affection dear,
A welcome give more kind and true, 510
Than aught my better fortunes knew.
Forgive, my friend, a father's boast;
O! it out-beggars all I lost!"

XXIV.

Delightful praise! — like summer rose,
That brighter in the dew-drop glows,
The bashful maiden's cheek appear'd,
For Douglas spoke, and Malcolm heard.
The flush of shame-faced joy to hide,
The hounds, the hawk, her cares divide;
The loved caresses of the maid 520
The dogs with crouch and whimper paid
And, at her whistle, on her hand
The falcon took his favorite stand,
Closed his dark wing, relax'd his eye,
Nor, though unhooded, sought to fly.
And, trust, while in such guise she stood,
Like fabled Goddess of the wood,
That if a father's partial thought
O'erweigh'd her worth and beauty aught,
Well might the lover's judgment fail 530
To balance with a juster scale;
For with each secret glance he stole,
The fond enthusiast sent his soul.

XXV.

Of stature fair, and slender frame,
But firmly knit, was Malcolm Græme.
The belted plaid and tartan hose
Did ne'er more graceful limbs disclose;
His flaxen hair, of sunny hue,
Curl'd closely round his bonnet blue.
Train'd to the chase, his eagle eye   540
The ptarmigan in snow could spy:
Each pass, by mountain, lake, and heath,
He knew, through Lennox and Menteith;
Vain was the bound of dark-brown doe,
When Malcolm bent his sounding bow,
And scarce that doe, though wing'd with fear,
Outstripp'd in speed the mountaineer:
Right up Ben-Lomond could he press,
And not a sob his toil confess.
His form accorded with a mind   550
Lively and ardent, frank and kind;
A blither heart, till Ellen came,
Did never love nor sorrow tame;
It danced as lightsome in his breast,
As play'd the feather on his crest.
Yet friends, who nearest knew the youth,
His scorn of wrong, his zeal for truth,
And bards, who saw his features bold,
When kindled by the tales of old,

THE ISLAND. 67

Said, were that youth to manhood grown, 560
Not long should Roderick Dhu's renown
Be foremost voiced by mountain fame,
But quail to that of Malcolm Græme.

XXVI.

Now back they wend their watery way,
And, "O my sire!" did Ellen say,
"Why urge thy chase so far astray?
And why so late return'd? And why"—
The rest was in her speaking eye.
"My child, the chase I follow far,
'Tis mimicry of noble war; 570
And with that gallant pastime reft
Were all of Douglas I have left.
I met young Malcolm as I stray'd
Far eastward, in Glenfinlas' shade,
Nor stray'd I safe; for, all around,
Hunters and horsemen scour'd the ground.
This youth, though still a royal ward,
Risk'd life and land to be my guard,
And through the passes of the wood
Guided my steps, not unpursued; 580
And Roderick shall his welcome make,
Despite old spleen, for Douglas' sake.
Then must he seek Strath-Endrick glen,
Nor peril aught for me agen."

XXVII.

Sir Roderick, who to meet them came,
Redden'd at sight of Malcolm Græme,
Yet, not in action, word, or eye,
Fail'd aught in hospitality.
In talk and sport they whiled away
The morning of that summer day; 590
But at high noon a courier light
Held secret parley with the knight,
Whose moody aspect soon declared,
That evil were the news he heard.
Deep thought seem'd toiling in his head;
Yet was the evening banquet made,
Ere he assembled round the flame,
His mother, Douglas, and the Græme,
And Ellen too; then cast around
His eyes, then fix'd them on the ground, 600
As studying phrase that might avail
Best to convey unpleasant tale.
Long with his dagger's hilt he play'd,
Then raised his haughty brow, and said: —

XXVIII.

"Short be my speech; — nor time affords,
Nor my plain temper, glozing words.
Kinsman and father, — if such name
Douglas vouchsafe to Roderick's claim;

Mine honor'd mother; — Ellen — why,
My cousin, turn away thine eye? —
And Græme; in whom I hope to know
Full soon a noble friend or foe,
When age shall give thee thy command,
And leading in thy native land, —
List all! — The King's vindictive pride
Boasts to have tamed the Border-side,
Where chiefs, with hound and hawk who came
To share their monarch's sylvan game,
Themselves in bloody toils were snared;
And when the banquet they prepared,
And wide their loyal portals flung,
O'er their own gateway struggling hung.
Loud cries their blood from Meggat's mead,
From Yarrow braes, and banks of Tweed,
Where the lone streams of Ettrick glide,
And from the silver Teviot's side;
The dales, where martial clans did ride,
Are now one sheep-walk, waste and wide.
This tyrant of the Scottish throne,
So faithless, and so ruthless known,
Now hither comes; his end the same,
The same pretext of sylvan game.
What grace for Highland Chiefs, judge ye
By fate of Border chivalry.
Yet more; amid Glenfinlas green,

Douglas, thy stately form was seen.
This by espial sure I know:
Your counsel in the streight I show."—

XXIX.

Ellen and Margaret fearfully
Sought comfort in each other's eye,
Then turn'd their ghastly look, each one,
This to her sire, that to her son.
The hasty color went and came
In the bold cheek of Malcolm Græme,
But from his glance it well appear'd,
'Twas but for Ellen that he fear'd;
While, sorrowful, but undismay'd,
The Douglas thus his counsel said:
"Brave Roderick, though the tempest roar,
It may but thunder and pass o'er;
Nor will I here remain an hour,
To draw the lightning on thy bower;
For well thou know'st, at this gray head
The royal bolt were fiercest sped.
For thee, who, at thy King's command,
Canst aid him with a gallant band,
Submission, homage, humbled pride,
Shall turn the monarch's wrath aside.
Poor remnants of the Bleeding Heart,
Ellen and I will seek, apart,

THE ISLAND. 71

The refuge of some forest cell,
There, like the hunted quarry, dwell,
Till, on the mountain and the moor,
The stern pursuit be pass'd and o'er."—

XXX.

"No, by mine honor," Roderick said,
"So help me Heaven, and my good blade!
No, never! Blasted be yon Pine,
My father's ancient crest, and mine,
If from its shade in danger part
The lineage of the Bleeding Heart! 670
Hear my blunt speech: grant me this maid
To wife, thy counsel to mine aid;
To Douglas, leagued with Roderick Dhu,
Will friends and allies flock enow;
Like cause of doubt, distrust, and grief,
Will bind to us each Western Chief.
When the loud pipes my bridal tell,
The Links of Forth shall hear the knell,
The guards shall start in Stirling's porch;
And, when I light the nuptial torch, 680
A thousand villages in flames
Shall scare the slumbers of King James!
— Nay, Ellen, blench not thus away,
And, mother, cease these signs, I pray;
I meant not all my heart might say.—

Small need of inroad, or of fight,
When the sage Douglas may unite
Each mountain clan in friendly band,
To guard the passes of their land,
Till the foil'd king, from pathless glen, 690
Shall bootless turn him home agen."

XXXI.

There are who have, at midnight hour,
In slumber scaled a dizzy tower,
And, on the verge that beetled o'er
The ocean tide's incessant roar,
Dream'd calmly out their dangerous dream,
Till waken'd by the morning beam;
When dazzled by the eastern glow,
Such startler cast his glance below,
And saw unmeasured depth around, 700
And heard unintermitted sound,
And thought the battled fence so frail,
It waved like cobweb in the gale; —
Amid his senses' giddy wheel,
Did he not desperate impulse feel,
Headlong to plunge himself below,
And meet the worst his fears foreshow? —
Thus, Ellen, dizzy and astound,
As sudden ruin yawn'd around,
By crossing terrors wildly toss'd, 710

Still for the Douglas fearing most,
Could scarce the desperate thought withstand,
To buy his safety with her hand.

XXXII.

Such purpose dread could Malcolm spy
In Ellen's quivering lip and eye,
And eager rose to speak — but ere
His tongue could hurry forth his fear,
Had Douglas mark'd the hectic strife,
Where death seem'd combating with life;
For to her cheek, in feverish flood, 720
One instant rush'd the throbbing blood,
Then ebbing back, with sudden sway,
Left its domain as wan as clay.
"Roderick, enough! enough!" he cried,
"My daughter cannot be thy bride;
Not that the blush to wooer dear,
Nor paleness that of maiden fear.
It may not be — forgive her, Chief,
Nor hazard aught for our relief.
Against his sovereign, Douglas ne'er 730
Will level a rebellious spear.
'Twas I that taught his youthful hand
To rein a steed and wield a brand;
I see him yet, the princely boy!
Not Ellen more my pride and joy;

I love him still, despite my wrongs,
By hasty wrath, and slanderous tongues.
O seek the grace you well may find,
Without a cause to mine combined."

XXXIII.

Twice through the hall the Chieftain strode; 740
The waving of his tartans broad,
And darken'd brow, where wounded pride
With ire and disappointment vied,
Seem'd, by the torch's gloomy light,
Like the ill Demon of the night,
Stooping his pinions' shadowy sway
Upon the nighted pilgrim's way:
But, unrequited Love! thy dart
Plunged deepest its envenom'd smart,
And Roderick, with thine anguish stung, 750
At length the hand of Douglas wrung,
While eyes, that mock'd at tears before,
With bitter drops were running o'er.
The death-pangs of long-cherish'd hope
Scarce in that ample breast had scope,
But, struggling with his spirit proud,
Convulsive heaved its chequer'd shroud,
While every sob — so mute were all —
Was heard distinctly through the hall.
The son's despair, the mother's look 760

Ill might the gentle Ellen brook;
She rose, and to her side there came,
To aid her parting steps, the Græme.

XXXIV.

Then Roderick from the Douglas broke —
As flashes flame through sable smoke,
Kindling its wreaths, long, dark, and low,
To one broad blaze of ruddy glow,
So the deep anguish of despair
Burst, in fierce jealousy, to air.
With stalwart grasp his hand he laid 770
On Malcolm's breast and belted plaid:
"Back, beardless boy!" he sternly said,
"Back, minion! hold'st thou thus at naught
The lesson I so lately taught?
This roof, the Douglas, and that maid,
Thank thou for punishment delay'd."
Eager as greyhound on his game,
Fiercely with Roderick grappled Græme.
"Perish my name, if aught afford
Its Chieftain safety, save his sword!" 780
Thus as they strove, their desperate hand
Griped to the dagger or the brand,
And death had been — but Douglas rose,
And thrust between the struggling foes
His giant strength: — "Chieftains, forego!

I hold the first who strikes, my foe. —
Madmen, forbear your frantic jar!
What! is the Douglas fall'n so far,
His daughter's hand is deem'd the spoil
Of such dishonorable broil!" 790
Sullen and slowly, they unclasp,
As struck with shame, their desperate grasp,
And each upon his rival glared,
With foot advanced, and blade half bared.

XXXV.

Ere yet the brands aloft were flung,
Margaret on Roderick's mantle hung,
And Malcolm heard his Ellen's scream,
As falter'd through terrific dream.
Then Roderick plunged in sheath his sword,
And veil'd his wrath in scornful word: 800
"Rest safe till morning; pity 'twere
Such cheek should feel the midnight air!
Then mayest thou to James Stuart tell,
Roderick will keep the lake and fell,
Nor lackey, with his freeborn clan,
The pageant pomp of earthly man.
More would he of Clan-Alpine know,
Thou canst our strength and passes show. —
Malise, what ho!" — his henchman came;
"Give our safe-conduct to the Græme." 810

Young Malcolm answer'd, calm and bold,
"Fear nothing for thy favorite hold;
The spot an angel deign'd to grace
Is bless'd, though robbers haunt the place.
Thy churlish courtesy for those
Reserve who fear to be thy foes.
As safe to me the mountain way
At midnight as in blaze of day,
Though with his boldest at his back,
Even Roderick Dhu beset the track. — 820
Brave Douglas, — lovely Ellen, — nay,
Naught here of parting will I say.
Earth does not hold a lonesome glen,
So secret, but we meet agen. —
Chieftain! we too shall find an hour" —
He said, and left the sylvan bower.

XXXVI.

Old Allan follow'd to the strand,
(Such was the Douglas's command,)
And anxious told, how, on the morn,
The stern Sir Roderick deep had sworn, 830
The Fiery Cross should circle o'er
Dale, glen, and valley, down, and moor.
Much were the peril to the Græme,
From those who to the signal came;
Far up the lake 'twere safest land,

Himself would row him to the strand.
He gave his counsel to the wind,
While Malcolm did, unheeding, bind,
Round dirk and pouch and broadsword roll'd,
His ample plaid in tighten'd fold,   840
And stripp'd his limbs to such array,
As best might suit the watery way.

XXXVII.

Then spoke abrupt: "Farewell to thee,
Pattern of old fidelity!"
The Minstrel's hand he kindly press'd, —
"O! could I point a place of rest!
My sovereign holds in ward my land,
My uncle leads my vassal band;
To tame his foes, his friends to aid,
Poor Malcolm has but heart and blade.   850
Yet, if there be one faithful Græme,
Who loves the Chieftain of his name,
Not long shall honor'd Douglas dwell,
Like hunted stag in mountain cell;
Nor, ere yon pride-swoll'n robber dare, —
I may not give the rest to air!
Tell Roderick Dhu, I owed him naught,
Not the poor service of a boat,
To waft me to yon mountain-side." —
Then plunged he in the flashing tide.   860

Bold o'er the flood his head he bore,
And stoutly steer'd him from the shore;
And Allan strain'd his anxious eye,
Far 'mid the lake his form to spy.
Darkening across each puny wave,
To which the moon her silver gave,
Fast as the cormorant could skim,
The swimmer plied each active limb;
Then landing in the moonlight dell,
Loud shouted of his weal to tell.
The Minstrel heard the far halloo,
And joyful from the shore withdrew.

CANTO THIRD.

The Gathering.

I.

TIME rolls his ceaseless course. The race of yore,
  Who danced our infancy upon their knee,
And told our marvelling boyhood legends store
  Of their strange ventures happ'd by land or sea,
How are they blotted from the things that be!
  How few, all weak and wither'd of their force,
Wait on the verge of dark eternity,
  Like stranded wrecks, the tide returning hoarse,
To sweep them from our sight! Time rolls his ceaseless
      course.

Yet live there still who can remember well,   10
  How, when a mountain chief his bugle blew,
Both field and forest, dingle, cliff, and dell,
  And solitary heath, the signal knew;
And fast the faithful clan around him drew,
  What time the warning note was keenly wound,
What time aloft their kindred banner flew,
  While clamorous war-pipes yell'd the gathering sound,
And while the Fiery Cross glanced, like a meteor, round.

II.

The Summer dawn's reflected hue
To purple changed Loch Katrine blue; 20
Mildly and soft the western breeze
Just kiss'd the lake, just stirr'd the trees,
And the pleased lake, like maiden coy,
Trembled but dimpled not for joy;
The mountain-shadows on her breast
Were neither broken nor at rest;
In bright uncertainty they lie,
Like future joys to Fancy's eye.
The water-lily to the light
Her chalice rear'd of silver bright; 30
The doe awoke, and to the lawn,
Begemm'd with dewdrops, led her fawn;
The gray mist left the mountain side,
The torrent show'd its glistening pride;
Invisible in flecked sky,
The lark sent down her revelry;
The blackbird and the speckled thrush
Good-morrow gave from brake and bush;
In answer coo'd the cushat dove
Her notes of peace, and rest, and love. 40

III.

No thought of peace, no thought of rest,
Assuaged the storm in Roderick's breast.

With sheathed broadsword in his hand,
Abrupt he paced the islet strand,
And eyed the rising sun, and laid
His hand on his impatient blade.
Beneath a rock, his vassals' care
Was prompt the ritual to prepare,
With deep and deathful meaning fraught;
For such Antiquity had taught   50
Was preface meet, ere yet abroad
The Cross of Fire should take its road.
The shrinking band stood oft aghast
At the impatient glance he cast; —
Such glance the mountain eagle threw,
As, from the cliffs of Benvenue,
She spread her dark sails on the wind,
And, high in middle heaven reclined,
With her broad shadow on the lake,
Silenced the warblers of the brake.   60

IV.

A heap of wither'd boughs was piled,
Of juniper and rowan wild,
Mingled with shivers from the oak,
Rent by the lightning's recent stroke.
Brian, the Hermit, by it stood,
Barefooted, in his frock and hood.
His grisled beard and matted hair

Obscured a visage of despair;
His naked arms and legs, seam'd o'er,
The scars of frantic penance bore.
That monk, of savage form and face,
The impending danger of his race
Had drawn from deepest solitude,
Far in Benharrow's bosom rude.
Not his the mien of Christian priest,
But Druid's, from the grave released,
Whose harden'd heart and eye might brook
On human sacrifice to look;
And much, 'twas said, of heathen lore
Mix'd in the charms he mutter'd o'er.
The hallow'd creed gave only worse
And deadlier emphasis of curse;
No peasant sought that Hermit's prayer,
His cave the pilgrim shunn'd with care,
The eager huntsman knew his bound,
And in mid chase call'd off his hound;
Or if, in lonely glen or strath,
The desert-dweller met his path,
He pray'd, and sign'd the cross between,
While terror took devotion's mien.

V.

Of Brian's birth strange tales were told.
His mother watch'd a midnight fold,

Built deep within a dreary glen,
Where scatter'd lay the bones of men,
In some forgotten battle slain,
And bleach'd by drifting wind and rain.
It might have tamed a warrior's heart,
To view such mockery of his art!
The knot-grass fetter'd there the hand,
Which once could burst an iron band; 100
Beneath the broad and ample bone,
That buckler'd heart to fear unknown,
A feeble and a timorous guest,
The field-fare framed her lowly nest;
There the slow blind-worm left his slime
On the fleet limbs that mock'd at time;
And there, too, lay the leader's skull,
Still wreath'd with chaplet, flush'd and full,
For heath-bell, with her purple bloom,
Supplied the bonnet and the plume. 110
All night, in this sad glen, the maid
Sate, shrouded in her mantle's shade;
— She said, no shepherd sought her side,
No hunter's hand her snood untied,
Yet ne'er again to braid her hair
The virgin snood did Alice wear;
Gone was her maiden glee and sport,
Her maiden girdle all too short,
Nor sought she, from that fatal night,

Or holy church or blessed rite, 120
But locked her secret in her breast,
And died in travail, unconfess'd.

VI.

Alone, among his young compeers,
Was Brian from his infant years;
A moody and heart-broken boy,
Estranged from sympathy and joy,
Bearing each taunt which careless tongue
On his mysterious lineage flung.
Whole nights he spent by moonlight pale,
To wood and stream his hap to wail, 130
Till, frantic, he as truth received
What of his birth the crowd believed,
And sought, in mist and meteor fire,
To meet and know his Phantom Sire!
In vain, to soothe his wayward fate,
The cloister oped her pitying gate;
In vain, the learning of the age
Unclasp'd the sable-letter'd page;
Even in its treasures he could find
Food for the fever of his mind. 140
Eager he read whatever tells
Of magic, cabala, and spells,
And every dark pursuit allied
To curious and presumptuous pride;

Till, with fired brain and nerves o'erstrung,
And heart with mystic horrors wrung,
Desperate he sought Benharrow's den,
And hid him from the haunts of men.

VII.

The desert gave him visions wild,
Such as might suit the spectre's child. 150
Where with black cliffs the torrents toil,
He watch'd the wheeling eddies boil,
Till, from their foam, his dazzled eyes
Beheld the River Demon rise;
The mountain mist took form and limb,
Of noontide hag, or goblin grim;
The midnight wind came wild and dread,
Swell'd with the voices of the dead;
Far on the future battle-heath
His eye beheld the ranks of death: 160
Thus the lone Seer, from mankind hurl'd,
Shaped forth a disembodied world.
One lingering sympathy of mind
Still bound him to the mortal kind;
The only parent he could claim
Of ancient Alpine lineage came.
Late had he heard, in prophet's dream,
The fatal Ben-Shie's boding scream;
Sounds, too, had come in midnight blast,

Of charging steeds, careering fast 170
Along Benharrow's shingly side,
Where mortal horseman ne'er might ride;
The thunderbolt had split the pine, —
All augur'd ill to Alpine's line.
He girt his loins, and came to show
The signals of impending woe,
And now stood prompt to bless or ban,
As bade the Chieftain of his clan.

VIII.

'Twas all prepared; — and from the rock,
A goat, the patriarch of the flock, 180
Before the kindling pile was laid,
And pierced by Roderick's ready blade.
Patient the sickening victim eyed
The life-blood ebb in crimson tide,
Down his clogg'd beard and shaggy limb,
Till darkness glazed his eyeballs dim.
The grisly priest, with murmuring prayer,
A slender crosslet form'd with care,
A cubit's length in measure due;
The shaft and limbs were rods of yew, 190
Whose parents in Inch-Cailliach wave
Their shadows o'er Clan-Alpine's grave,
And, answering Lomond's breezes deep,
Soothe many a chieftain's endless sleep.

The Cross, thus form'd, he held on high,
With wasted hand, and haggard eye,
And strange and mingled feelings woke,
While his anathema he spoke:

IX.

" Woe to the clansman, who shall view
This symbol of sepulchral yew, 200
Forgetful that its branches grew
Where weep the heavens their holiest dew
   On Alpine's dwelling low!
Deserter of his Chieftain's trust,
He ne'er shall mingle with their dust,
But, from his sires and kindred thrust,
Each clansman's execration just
   Shall doom him wrath and woe."
He paused;— the word the vassals took,
With forward step and fiery look, 210
On high their naked brands they shook,
Their clattering targets wildly strook;
   And first in murmur low,
Then, like the billow in his course,
That far to seaward finds his source,
And flings to shore his muster'd force,
Burst, with loud roar, their answer hoarse,
   " Woe to the traitor, woe!"
Ben-an's gray scalp the accents knew,

The joyous wolf from covert drew,
The exulting eagle scream'd afar,—
They knew the voice of Alpine's war.

X.

The shout was hush'd on lake and fell,
The Monk resumed his mutter'd spell:
Dismal and low its accents came,
The while he scathed the Cross with flame;
And the few words that reach'd the air,
Although the holiest name was there,
Had more of blasphemy than prayer.
But when he shook above the crowd
Its kindled points, he spoke aloud:
"Woe to the wretch who fails to rear
At this dread sign the ready spear!
For, as the flames this symbol sear,
His home, the refuge of his fear,
  A kindred fate shall know;
Far o'er its roof the volumed flame
Clan-Alpine's vengeance shall proclaim,
While maids and matrons on his name
Shall call down wretchedness and shame,
  And infamy and woe."—
Then rose the cry of females, shrill
As goss-hawk's whistle on the hill,
Denouncing misery and ill,

Mingled with childhood's babbling trill
  Of curses stammer'd slow;
Answering, with imprecation dread,
"Sunk be his home in embers red!
And cursed be the meanest shed
That e'er shall hide the houseless head   250
  We doom to want and woe!"
A sharp and shrieking echo gave,
Coir-Uriskin, thy goblin cave!
And the gray pass where birches wave
  On Beala-nam-bo.

XI.

Then deeper paused the priest anew,
And hard his laboring breath he drew,
While, with set teeth and clenched hand,
And eyes that glow'd like fiery brand,
He meditated curse more dread,   260
And deadlier, on the clansman's head,
Who, summon'd to his Chieftain's aid
The signal saw and disobey'd.
The crosslet's points of sparkling wood,
He quench'd among the bubbling blood,
And, as again the sign he rear'd,
Hollow and hoarse his voice was heard:
"When flits this Cross from man to man,
Vich-Alpine's summons to his clan,

Burst be the ear that fails to heed! 270
Palsied the foot that shuns to speed!
May ravens tear the careless eyes,
Wolves make the coward heart their prize!
As sinks that blood-stream in the earth,
So may his heart's-blood drench his hearth!
As dies in hissing gore the spark,
Quench thou his light, Destruction dark!
And be the grace to him denied,
Bought by this sign to all beside!"
He ceased; no echo gave agen 280
The murmur of the deep Amen.

XII.

Then Roderick, with impatient look,
From Brian's hand the symbol took:
"Speed, Malise, speed!" he said, and gave
The crosslet to his henchman brave.
"The muster-place be Lanrick mead —
Instant the time — speed, Malise, speed!"
Like heath-bird, when the hawks pursue,
A barge across Loch Katrine flew; .
High stood the henchman on the prow, 290
So rapidly the barge-men row,
The bubbles, where they launch'd the boat,
Were all unbroken and afloat,
Dancing in foam and ripple still,

When it had near'd the mainland hill;
And from the silver beach's side
Still was the prow three fathom wide
When lightly bounded to the land
The messenger of blood and brand.

XIII.

Speed, Malise, speed! the dun deer's hide 300
On fleeter foot was never tied.
Speed, Malise, speed! such cause of haste
Thine active sinews never braced.
Bend 'gainst the steepy hill thy breast,
Burst down like torrent from its crest;
With short and springing footstep pass
The trembling bog and false morass;
Across the brook like roebuck bound,
And thread the brake like questing hound;
The crag is high, the scaur is deep, 310
Yet shrink not from the desperate leap:
Parch'd are thy burning lips and brow,
Yet by the fountain pause not now;
Herald of battle, fate, and fear,
Stretch onward in thy fleet career!
The wounded hind thou track'st not now,
Pursuest not maid through greenwood bough,
Nor pliest thou now thy flying pace,
With rivals in the mountain race;

But danger, death, and warrior deed,   230
Are in thy course — speed, Malise, speed!

XIV.

Fast as the fatal symbol flies,
In arms the huts and hamlets rise;
From winding glen, from upland brown,
They pour'd each hardy tenant down.
Nor slack'd the messenger his pace;
He show'd the sign, he named the place,
And, pressing forward like the wind,
Left clamor and surprise behind.
The fisherman forsook the strand,   330
The swarthy smith took dirk and brand;
With changed cheer, the mower blithe
Left in the half-cut swathe the scythe;
The herds without a keeper stray'd,
The plough was in mid-furrow stay'd,
The falc'ner toss'd his hawk away,
The hunter left the stag at bay;
Prompt at the signal of alarms,
Each son of Alpine rush'd to arms;
So swept the tumult and affray   340
Along the margin of Achray.
Alas, thou lovely lake! that e'er
Thy banks should echo sounds of fear!
The rocks, the bosky thickets, sleep

So stilly on thy bosom deep,
The lark's blithe carol, from the cloud,
Seems for the scene too gail- loud.

XV.

Speed, Malise, speed! The lake is past,
Duncraggan's huts appear at last,
And peep, like moss-grown rocks, half seen,   350
Half hidden in the copse so green;
There mayst thou rest, thy labor done,
Their Lord shall speed the signal on. —
As stoops the hawk upon his prey,
The henchman shot him down the way.
— What woful accents load the gale?
The funeral yell, the female wail!
A gallant hunter's sport is o'er,
A valiant warrior fights no more.
Who, in the battle or the chase,   360
At Roderick's side shall fill his place! —
Within the hall, where torches' ray
Supplies the excluded beams of day,
Lies Duncan on his lowly bier,
And o'er him streams his widow's tear.
His stripling son stands mournful by,
His youngest weeps, but knows not why;
The village maids and matrons round
The dismal coronach resound.

XXI.

Coronach.

He is gone on the mountain,
    He is lost to the forest,
Like a summer-dried fountain,
    When our need was the sorest.
The font, reappearing,
    From the raindrops shall borrow,
But to us comes no cheering,
    To Duncan no morrow!

The hand of the reaper
    Takes the ears that are hoary,
But the voice of the weeper
    Wails manhood in glory.
The autumn winds rushing
    Wafts the leaves that are searest,
But our flower was in flushing,
    When blighting was nearest.

Fleet foot on the correi,
    Sage counsel in cumber,
Red hand in the foray,
    How sound is thy slumber!
Like the dew on the mountain,
    Like the foam on the river,
Like the bubble on the fountain
    Thou art gone, and forever!

XVII.

See Stumah, who, the bier beside,
His master's corpse with wonder eyed,
Poor Stumah! whom his least halloo
Could send like lightning o'er the dew,
Bristles his crest, and points his ears,
As if some stranger step he hears.
'Tis not a mourner's muffled tread,   400
Who comes to sorrow o'er the dead,
But headlong haste, or deadly fear,
Urge the precipitate career.
All stand aghast : — unheeding all,
The henchman bursts into the hall ;
Before the dead man's bier he stood ;
Held forth the Cross besmear'd with blood ;
"The muster-place is Lanrick mead ;
Speed forth the signal! clansmen, speed!"

XVIII.

Angus, the heir of Duncan's line,   410
Sprung forth and seized the fatal sign.
In haste the stripling to his side
His father's dirk and broadsword tied ;
But when he saw his mother's eye
Watch him in speechless agony,
Back to her open'd arms he flew,

THE GATHERING.

Press'd on her lips a fond adieu —
"Alas!" she sobb'd, — "and yet be gone,
And speed thee forth, like Duncan's son!"
One look he cast upon the bier, 420
Dash'd from his eye the gathering tear,
Breathed deep, to clear his laboring breast,
And toss'd aloft his bonnet crest,
Then, like the high-bred colt, when, freed,
First he essays his fire and speed,
He vanish'd, and o'er moor and moss
Sped forward with the Fiery Cross.
Suspended was the widow's tear,
While yet his footsteps she could hear;
And when she mark'd the henchman's eye 430
Wet with unwonted sympathy,
"Kinsman," she said, "his race is run,
That should have sped thine errand on;
The oak has fall'n, — the sapling bough
Is all Duncraggan's shelter now.
Yet trust I well, his duty done,
The orphan's God will guard my son. —
And you, in many a danger true,
At Duncan's hest your blades that drew,
To arms, and guard that orphan's head! 440
Let babes and women wail the dead."
Then weapon-clang, and martial call,
Resounded through the funeral hall,

While from the walls the attendant band
Snatch'd sword and targe, with hurried hand;
And short and flitting energy
Glanced from the mourner's sunken eye,
As if the sounds to warrior dear
Might rouse her Duncan from his bier.
But faded soon that borrow'd force; 450
Grief claim'd his right, and tears their course.

XIX.

Benledi saw the Cross of Fire,
It glanced like lightning up Strath-Ire.
O'er dale and hill the summons flew,
Nor rest nor pause young Angus knew;
The tear that gather'd in his eye
He left the mountain-breeze to dry;
Until, where Teith's young waters roll,
Betwixt him and a wooded knoll,
That graced the sable strath with green, 460
The chapel of Saint Bride was seen.
Swoln was the stream, remote the bridge,
But Angus paused not on the edge;
Though the dark waves danced dizzily,
Though reel'd his sympathetic eye,
He dash'd amid the torrent's roar:
His right hand high the crosslet bore,
His left the pole-axe grasp'd, to guide

And stay his footing in the tide.
He stumbled twice — the foam splash'd high, 470
With hoarser swell the stream raced by;
And had he fall'n, — for ever there,
Farewell Duncraggan's orphan heir!
But still, as if in parting life,
Firmer he grasp'd the Cross of strife,
Until the opposing bank he gain'd,
And up the chapel pathway strain'd.

XX.

A blithesome rout, that morning tide,
Had sought the chapel of Saint Bride.
Her troth Tombea's Mary gave 480
To Norman, heir of Armandave,
And, issuing from the Gothic arch,
The bridal now resumed their march.
In rude, but glad procession, came
Bonneted sire and coif-clad dame;
And plaided youth, with jest and jeer,
Which snooded maiden would not hear:
And children, that, unwitting why,
Lent the gay shout their shrilly cry;
And minstrels, that in measures vied 490
Before the young and bonny bride,
Whose downcast eye and cheek disclose
The tear and blush of morning rose.

With virgin step, and bashful hand,
She held the kerchief's snowy band;
The gallant bridegroom by her side
Beheld his prize with victor's pride,
And the glad mother in her ear
Was closely whispering word of cheer.

XXI.

Who meets them at the churchyard gate?
The messenger of fear and fate!
Haste in his hurried accent lies,
And grief is swimming in his eyes.
All dripping from the recent flood,
Panting and travel-soil'd he stood,
The fatal sign of fire and sword
Held forth, and spoke the appointed word:
"The muster-place is Lanrick mead;
Speed forth the signal! Norman, speed!"
And must he change so soon the hand,
Just linked to his by holy band,
For the fell Cross of blood and brand?
And must the day, so blithe that rose,
And promised rapture in the close,
Before its setting hour divide
The bridegroom from the plighted bride?
O fatal doom! — it must! it must!

Clan-Alpine's cause, her Chieftain's trust,
Her summons dread, brook no delay;
Stretch to the race — away! away! 520

XXII.

Yet slow he laid his plaid aside,
And, lingering, eyed his lovely bride,
Until he saw the starting tear
Speak woe he might not stop to cheer;
Then, trusting not a second look,
In haste he sped him up the brook,
Nor backward glanced, till on the heath
Where Lubnaig's lake supplies the Teith.
— What in the racer's bosom stirr'd?
The sickening pang of hope deferr'd, 530
And memory, with a torturing train
Of all his morning visions vain.
Mingled with love's impatience, came
The manly thirst for martial fame;
The stormy joy of mountaineers,
Ere yet they rush upon the spears;
And zeal for Clan and Chieftain burning,
And hope, from well-fought field returning,
With war's red honors on his crest,
To clasp his Mary to his breast. 540
Stung by such thoughts, o'er bank and brae,
Like fire from flint he glanced away,

While high resolve, and feeling strong,
Burst into voluntary song.

XXIII.

Song.

The heath this night must be my bed,
The bracken curtain for my head,
My lullaby the warder's tread,
    Far, far, from love and thee, Mary;
To-morrow eve, more stilly laid,
My couch may be my bloody plaid,   550
My vesper song, thy wail, sweet maid!
    It will not waken me, Mary!

I may not, dare not, fancy now
The grief that clouds thy lovely brow,
I dare not think upon thy vow,
    And all it promised me, Mary!
No fond regret must Norman know;
When bursts Clan-Alpine on the foe,
His heart must be like bended bow,
    His foot like arrow free, Mary.   560

A time will come with feeling fraught,
For, if I fall in battle fought,
Thy hapless lover's dying thought
    Shall be a thought on thee, Mary.

And if return'd from conquer'd foes,
How blithely will the evening close,
How sweet the linnet sing repose,
    To my young bride and me, Mary!

XXIV.

Not faster o'er thy heathery braes,
Balquidder, speeds the midnight blaze,   570
Rushing, in conflagration strong,
Thy deep ravines and dells along,
Wrapping thy cliffs in purple glow,
And reddening the dark lakes below;
Nor faster speeds it, nor so far,
As o'er thy heaths the voice of war.
The signal roused to martial coil
The sullen margin of Loch Voil,
Waked still Loch Doine, and to the source
Alarm'd, Balvaig, thy swampy course;   580
Thence southward turn'd its rapid road
Adown Strath-Gartney's valley broad,
Till rose in arms each man might claim
A portion in Clan-Alpine's name,
From the gray sire, whose trembling hand
Could hardly buckle on his brand,
To the raw boy, whose shaft and bow
Were yet scarce terror to the crow.

Each valley, each sequester'd glen,
Muster'd its little horde of men, 590
That met as torrents from the height
In Highland dale their streams unite,
Still gathering, as they pour along,
A voice more loud, a tide more strong,
Till at the rendezvous they stood
By hundreds prompt for blows and blood,
Each train'd to arms since life began,
Owning no tie but to his clan,
No oath, but by his chieftain's hand,
No law, but Roderick Dhu's command. 600

XXV.

That summer morn had Roderick Dhu
Survey'd the skirts of Bevenue,
And sent his scouts o'er hill and heath,
To view the frontiers of Menteith.
All backward came with news of truce;
Still lay each martial Græme and Bruce,
In Rednock courts no horsemen wait,
No banner waved on Cardross gate,
On Duchray's towers no beacon shone,
Nor scared the herons from Loch Con; 610
All seem'd at peace. — Now wot ye why
The Chieftain, with such anxious eye,

Ere to the muster he repair,
This western frontier scann'd with care ? —
In Benvenue's most darksome cleft,
A fair, though cruel, pledge was left;
For Douglas, to his promise true,
That morning from the isle withdrew,
And in a deep sequester'd dell
Had sought a low and lonely cell.   620
By many a bard, in Celtic tongue,
Has Coir-nan-Uriskin been sung;
A softer name the Saxons gave,
And called the grot the Goblin Cave.

XXVI.

It was a wild and strange retreat,
As e'er was trod by outlaw's feet.
The dell, upon the mountain's crest,
Yawn'd like a gash on warrior's breast
Its trench had staid full many a rock,
Hurl'd by primeval earthquake shock   630
From Benvenue's gray summit wild,
And here, in random ruin piled,
They frown'd incumbent o'er the spot,
And form'd the rugged sylvan grot.
The oak and birch, with mingled shade,
At noontide there a twilight made,

Unless when short and sudden shone
Some straggling beam on cliff or stone,
With such a glimpse as prophet's eye
Gains on thy depth, Futurity. 640
No murmur waked the solemn still,
Save tinkling of a fountain rill;
But when the wind chafed with the lake,
A sullen sound would upward break,
With dashing hollow voice, that spoke
The incessant war of wave and rock.
Suspended cliffs, with hideous sway,
Seem'd nodding o'er the cavern gray.
From such a den the wolf had sprung,
In such the wildcat leaves her young; 650
Yet Douglas and his daughter fair
Sought for a space their safety there.
Gray Superstition's whisper dread
Debarr'd the spot to vulgar tread;
For there, she said, did fays resort,
And satyrs hold their sylvan court,
By moonlight tread the mystic maze,
And blast the rash beholder's gaze.

XXVII.

Now eve, with western shadows long,
Floated on Katrine bright and strong, 660

When Roderick, with a chosen few,
Repass'd the heights of Benvenue.
Above the Goblin-cave they go,
Through the wild pass of Beal-nam-bo;
The prompt retainers speed before,
To launch the shallop from the shore,
For 'cross Loch Katrine lies his way
To view the passes of Achray,
And place his clansmen in array.
Yet lags the chief in musing mind,   670
Unwonted sight, his men behind.
A single page, to bear his sword,
Alone attended on his lord;
The rest their way through thickets break,
And soon await him by the lake.
It was a fair and gallant sight,
To view them from the neighboring height,
By the low-levell'd sunbeam's light;
For strength and stature, from the clan
Each warrior was a chosen man,   680
As even afar might well be seen,
By their proud step and martial mien.
Their feathers dance, their tartans float,
Their targets gleam, as by the boat
A wild and warlike group they stand,
That well became such mountain strand.

XXVIII.

Their Chief, with step reluctant, still
Was lingering on the craggy hill,
Hard by where turn'd apart the road
To Douglas's obscure abode. 690
It was but with that dawning morn
That Roderick Dhu had proudly sworn
To drown his love in war's wild roar,
Nor think of Ellen Douglas more;
But he who stems a stream with sand,
And fetters flame with flaxen band,
Has yet a harder task to prove —
By firm resolve to conquer love!
Eve finds the Chief, like restless ghost,
Still hovering near his treasure lost; 700
For though his haughty heart deny
A parting meeting to his eye,
Still fondly strains his anxious ear,
The accents of her voice to hear,
And inly did he curse the breeze
That waked to sound the rustling trees.
But hark! what mingles in the strain?
It is the harp of Allan-bane,
That wakes its measure slow and high,
Attuned to sacred minstrelsy. 710
What melting voice attends the strings?
'Tis Ellen, or an angel, sings.

XXIX.

Hymn to the Virgin.

Ave Maria! maiden mild!
  Listen to a maiden's prayer!
Thou canst hear though from the wild,
  Thou canst save amid despair.
Safe may we sleep beneath thy care,
  Though banish'd, outcast, and reviled —
Maiden! hear a maiden's prayer;
  Mother, hear a suppliant child! 720
              Ave Maria!

Ave Maria! undefiled!
  The flinty couch we now must share
Shall seem with down of eider piled,
  If thy protection hover there.
The murky cavern's heavy air
  Shall breathe of balm if thou hast smiled;
Then, Maiden! hear a maiden's prayer,
  Mother, list a suppliant child!
              Ave Maria!

Ave Maria! Stainless styled!
  Foul demons of the earth and air, 730
From this their wonted haunt exiled,
  Shall flee before thy presence fair.

We bow us to our lot of care,
  Beneath thy guidance reconciled;
Hear for a maid a maiden's prayer,
  And for a father hear a child!
                    Ave Maria!

XXX.

Died on the harp the closing hymn —
Unmoved in attitude and limb,
As list'ning still, Clan-Alpine's lord
Stood leaning on his heavy sword,   740
Until the page, with humble sign,
Twice pointed to the sun's decline.
Then while his plaid he round him cast,
"It is the last time — 'tis the last,"
He mutter'd thrice, — "the last time e'er
That angel-voice shall Roderick hear!"
It was a goading thought — his stride
Hied hastier down the mountain-side;
Sullen he flung him in the boat,
An instant 'cross the lake it shot.   750
They landed in that silvery bay,
And eastward held their hasty way,
Till, with the latest beams of light,
The band arrived on Lanrick height,
Where muster'd in the vale below
Clan-Alpine's men in martial show.

XXXI.

A various scene the clansmen made,
Some sate, some stood, some slowly stray'd;
But most, with mantles folded round,
Were couch'd to rest upon the ground,   760
Scarce to be known by curious eye,
From the deep heather where they lie,
So well was match'd the tartan screen
*With heath-bell dark and brackens green;
Unless where, here and there, a blade,
Or lance's point, a glimmer made,
Like glow-worm twinkling through the shade.
But when, advancing through the gloom,
They saw the Chieftain's eagle plume,
Their shout of welcome, shrill and wide,   770
Shook the steep mountain's steady side.
Thrice it arose, and lake and fell
Three times return'd the martial yell;
It died upon Bochastle's plain,
And Silence claim'd her evening reign.

CANTO FOURTH.

The Prophecy.

I.

"THE rose is fairest wnen 'tis budding new,
   And hope is brightest when it dawns from fears;
The rose is sweetest wash'd with morning dew,
   And love is loveliest when embalmed in tears.
O wilding rose, whom fancy thus endears,
   I bid your blossoms in my bonnet wave,
Emblem of hope and love through future years!"
   Thus spoke young Norman, heir of Armandave,
What time the sun arose on Vennachar's broad wave.

II.

   Such fond conceit, half said, half sung,   10
   Love prompted to the bridegroom's tongue.
   All while he stripp'd the wild-rose spray,
   His axe and bow beside him lay,
   For on a pass 'twixt lake and wood,
   A wakeful sentinel he stood.
   Hark! — on the rock a footstep rung,

And instant to his arms he sprung.
"Stand, or thou diest!—What, Malise?— soon
Art thou return'd from Braes of Doune.
By thy keen step and glance I know   20
Thou bring'st us tidings of the foe."—
(For while the Fiery Cross hied on,
On distant scout had Malise gone.)
"Where sleeps the Chief?" the henchman said.
"Apart, in yonder misty glade;
To his lone couch I'll be your guide."—
Then call'd a slumberer by his side,
And stirr'd him with his slacken'd bow—
"Up, up, Glentarkin! rouse thee, ho!
We seek the Chieftain; on the track,   30
Keep eagle watch till I come back."

III.

Together up the pass they sped:
"What of the foemen?" Norman said.—
"Varying reports from near and far;
This certain,—that a band of war
Has for two days been ready boune,
At prompt command, to march from Doune;
King James, the while, with princely powers,
Holds revelry in Stirling towers.
Soon will this dark and gathering cloud   40

Speak on our glens in thunder loud.
Inured to bide such bitter bout,
The warrior's plaid may bear it out;
But, Norman, how wilt thou provide
A shelter for thy bonny bride?" —
"What! know ye not that Roderick's care
To the lone isle hath caused repair
Each maid and matron of the clan,
And every child and aged man
Unfit for arms? and given his charge, 50
Nor skiff nor shallop, boat nor barge,
Upon these lakes shall float at large,
But all beside the islet moor,
That such dear pledge may rest secure?" —

IV.

"'Tis well advised — the Chieftain's plan
Bespeaks the father of his clan.
But wherefore sleeps Sir Roderick Dhu
Apart from all his followers true?" —
"It is, because last evening-tide
Brian an augury hath tried, 60
Of that dread kind which must not be
Unless in dread extremity,
The Taghairm call'd; by which, afar,
Our sires foresaw the events of war.
Duncraggan's milk-white bull they slew."

MALISE.

"Ah! well the gallant brute I knew.
The choicest of the prey we had,
When swept our merry-men Gallangad.
His hide was snow, his horns were dark,
His red eye glow'd like fiery spark;   70
So fierce, so tameless, and so fleet,
Sore did he cumber our retreat,
And kept our stoutest kernes in awe,
Even at the pass of Beal 'maha.
But steep and flinty was the road,
And sharp the hurrying pikeman's goad,
And when we came to Dennan's Row,
A child might scatheless stroke his brow." —

V.

NORMAN.

" That bull was slain : his reeking hide
They stretch'd the cataract beside,   80
Whose waters their wild tumult toss
Adown the black and craggy boss
Of that huge cliff, whose ample verge
Tradition calls the Hero's Targe.
Couch'd on a shelf beneath its brink,
Close where the thundering torrents sink,
Rocking beneath their headlong sway,

And drizzled by the ceaseless spray,
Midst groan of rock, and roar of stream,
The wizard waits prophetic dream. 90
Nor distant rests the Chief; — but hush!
See, gliding slow through mist and bush,
The hermit gains yon rock, and stands
To gaze upon our slumbering bands.
Seems he not, Malise, like a ghost,
That hovers o'er a slaughter'd host?
Or raven on the blasted oak,
That, watching while the deer is broke,
His morsel claims with sullen croak?"

MALISE.

— " Peace! peace! to other than to me, 100
Thy words were evil augury;
But still I hold Sir Roderick's blade
Clan-Alpine's omen and her aid,
Not aught that, gleam'd from heaven or hell,
Yon fiend-begotten Monk can tell.
The Chieftain joins him, see — and now,
Together they descend the brow."

VI.

And, as they came, with Alpine's Lord
The Hermit Monk held solemn word:
" Roderick! it is a fearful strife, 110

For man endow'd with mortal life,
Whose shroud of sentient clay can still
Feel feverish pang and fainting chill,
Whose eye can stare in stony trance,
Whose hair can rouse like warrior's lance,
'Tis hard for such to view, unfurl'd,
The curtain of the future world.
Yet, witness every quaking limb,
My sunken pulse, my eyeballs dim,
My soul with harrowing anguish torn,
This for my Chieftain have I borne!—
The shapes that sought my fearful couch,
An human tongue may ne'er avouch;
No mortal man,— save he, who, bred
Between the living and the dead,
Is gifted beyond nature's law,—
Had e'er survived to say he saw.
At length the fateful answer came,
In characters of living flame!
Not spoke in word, nor blazed in scroll,
But borne and branded on my soul;—
WHICH SPILLS THE FOREMOST FOEMAN'S LIFE,
THAT PARTY CONQUERS IN THE STRIFE."—

VII.

"Thanks, Brian, for thy zeal and care!
Good is thine augury, and fair.

Clan-Alpine ne'er in battle stood,
But first our broadswords tasted blood.
A surer victim still I know,
Self-offer'd to the auspicious blow:
A spy has sought my land this morn, —   140
No eve shall witness his return!
My followers guard each pass's mouth,
To east, to westward, and to south;
Red Murdoch, bribed to be his guide,
Has charge to lead his steps aside,
Till, in deep path or dingle brown,
He light on those shall bring him down.
— But see, who comes his news to show!
Malise! what tidings of the foe?"

VIII.

"At Doune, o'er many a spear and glaive   150
Two Barons proud their banners wave.
I saw the Moray's silver star,
And mark'd the sable pale of Mar." —
"By Alpine's soul, high tidings those!
I love to hear of worthy foes.
When move they on?" — "To-morrow's noon
Will see them here for battle boune." —
"Then shall it see a meeting stern! —
But, for the place — say, couldst thou learn
Naught of the friendly clans of Earn?   160

Strengthened by them, we well might bide
The battle on Benledi's side.
Thou couldst not? — well! Clan-Alpine's men
Shall man the Trosachs' shaggy glen;
Within Loch Katrine's gorge we'll fight,
All in our maids' and matrons' sight,
Each for his hearth and household fire,
Father for child, and son for sire, —
Lover for maid beloved! — But why —
Is it the breeze affects mine eye? 170
Or dost thou come, ill-omen'd tear!
A messenger of doubt or fear?
No! sooner may the Saxon lance
Unfix Benledi from his stance,
Than doubt or terror can pierce through
The unyielding heart of Roderick Dhu!
'Tis stubborn as his trusty targe. —
Each to his post! — all know their charge."
The pibroch sounds, the bands advance,
The broadswords gleam, the banners dance, 180
Obedient to the Chieftain's glance. —
I turn me from the martial roar,
And seek Coir-Uriskin once more.

IX.

Where is the Douglas? — he is gone;
And Ellen sits on the gray stone

Fast by the cave, and makes her moan;
While vainly Allan's words of cheer
Are pour'd on her unheeding ear. —
"He will return — Dear lady, trust! —
With joy return; — he will — he must.   190
Well was it time to seek, afar,
Some refuge from impending war,
When e'en Clan-Alpine's rugged swarm
Are cow'd by the approaching storm.
I saw their boats, with many a light,
Floating the livelong yesternight,
Shifting like flashes darted forth
By the red streamers of the north;
I mark'd at morn how close they ride,
Thick moor'd by the lone islet's side,   200
Like wild ducks couching in the fen,
When stoops the hawk upon the glen.
Since this rude race dare not abide
The peril on the mainland side,
Shall not thy noble father's care
Some safe retreat for thee prepare?" —

X.

ELLEN.

No, Allan, no. Pretext so kind
My wakeful terrors could not blind.

THE PROPHECY.

When in such tender tone, yet grave,
Douglas a parting blessing gave,   210
The tear that glisten'd in his eye
Drown'd not his purpose fix'd on high.
My soul, though feminine and weak,
Can image his; e'en as the lake,
Itself disturb'd by slightest stroke,
Reflects the invulnerable rock.
He hears report of battle rife,
He deems himself the cause of strife.
I saw him redden, when the theme
Turn'd, Allan, on thine idle dream   220
Of Malcolm Græme, in fetters bound,
Which I, thou saidst, about him wound.
Think'st thou he trow'd thine omen aught?
Oh no! 'twas apprehensive thought
For the kind youth, — for Roderick too —
(Let me be just) that friend so true;
In danger both, and in our cause!
Minstrel, the Douglas dare not pause.
Why else that solemn warning given,
'If not on earth, we meet in heaven'?   230
Why else, to Cambus-kenneth's fane,
If eve return him not again,
Am I to hie, and make me known?
Alas! he goes to Scotland's throne,
Buys his friend's safety with his own; —

He goes to do — what I had done,
Had Douglas' daughter been his son!"

XI.

"Nay, lovely Ellen! — dearest, nay!
If aught should his return delay,
He only named yon holy fane 240
As fitting place to meet again.
Be sure he's safe; and for the Græme,
Heaven's blessing on his gallant name! —
My vision'd sight may yet prove true,
Nor bode of ill to him or you.
When did my gifted dream beguile?
Think of the stranger at the isle,
And think upon the harpings slow,
That presaged this approaching woe!
Sooth was my prophecy of fear; 250
Believe it when it augurs cheer.
Would we had left this dismal spot!
Ill luck still haunts a fairy grot.
Of such a wondrous tale I know —
Dear lady, change that look of woe,
My harp was wont thy grief to cheer." —

ELLEN.

"Well, be it as thou wilt; I hear,
But cannot stop the bursting tear."

The Minstrel tried his simple art,
But distant far was Ellen's heart. 260

XII.

Ballad.

ALICE BRAND.

Merry it is in the good greenwood,
　When the mavis and merle are singing,
When the deer sweeps by, and the hounds are in cry,
　And the hunter's horn is ringing.

"O Alice Brand, my native land
　Is lost for love of you;
And we must hold by wood and wold,
　As outlaws wont to do.

"O Alice, 'twas all for thy locks so bright,
　And 'twas all for thine eyes so blue, 270
That on the night of our luckless flight,
　Thy brother bold I slew.

"Now must I teach to hew the beech,
　The hand that held the glaive,
For leaves to spread our lowly bed,
　And stakes to fence our cave.

"And for vest of pall, thy fingers small,
  That wont on harp to stray,
A cloak must shear from the slaughter'd deer,
  To keep the cold away."   280

"O Richard! if my brother died,
  'Twas but a fatal chance;
For darkling was the battle tried,
  And fortune sped the lance.

"If pall and vair no more I wear,
  Nor thou the crimson sheen,
As warm, we'll say, is the russet gray,
  As gay the forest-green.

"And, Richard, if our lot be hard,
  And lost thy native land,   290
Still Alice has her own Richard,
  And he his Alice Brand."

XIII.

Ballad Continued.

'Tis merry, 'tis merry, in good greenwood,
  So blithe Lady Alice is singing;
On the beech's pride, and the oak's brown side,
  Lord Richard's axe is ringing.

Up spoke the moody Elfin King,
    Who won'd within the hill, —
Like wind in the porch of a ruin'd church,
    His voice was ghostly shrill.　　　　300

" Why sounds yon stroke on beech and oak,
    Our moonlight circle's screen ?
Or who comes here to chase the deer,
    Beloved of our Elfin Queen ?
Or who may dare on wold to wear
    The fairies' fatal green ?

" Up, Urgan, up! to yon mortal hie,
    For thou wert christen'd man ;
For cross or sign thou wilt not fly,
    For mutter'd word or ban.　　　　310

" Lay on him the curse of the wither'd heart,
    The curse of the sleepless eye ;
Till he wish and pray that his life would part,
    Not yet find leave to die."

XIV.

Ballad Continued.

'Tis merry, 'tis merry, in good greenwood,
    Though the birds have still'd their singing ;
The evening blaze doth Alice raise,
    And Richard is fagots bringing.

Up Urgan starts, that hideous dwarf,
  Before Lord Richard stands,   320
And, as he cross'd and bless'd himself,
"I fear not sign," quoth the grisly elf,
  "That is made with bloody hands."

But out then spoke she, Alice Brand,
  That woman void of fear, —
"And if there's blood upon his hand,
  'Tis but the blood of deer." —

"Now loud thou liest, thou bold of mood!
  It cleaves unto his hand,
The stain of thine own kindly blood,   330
  The blood of Ethert Brand." —

Then forward stepp'd she, Alice Brand,
  And made the holy sign, —
"And if there's blood on Richard's hand,
  A spotless hand is mine.

"And I conjure thee, Demon elf,
  By Him whom Demons fear,
To show us whence thou art thyself,
  And what thine errand here?"

XV.

Ballad Continued.

"'Tis merry, 'tis merry, in Fairy-land,   340
    When fairy birds are singing,
When the court doth ride by their monarch's side,
    With bit and bridle ringing:

"And gayly shines the Fairy-land —
    But all is glistening show
Like the idle gleam that December's beam
    Can dart on ice and snow.

"And fading, like that varied gleam,
    Is our inconstant shape,
Who now like knight and lady seem,   350
    And now like dwarf and ape.

"It was between the night and day,
    When the Fairy King has power,
That I sunk down in a sinful fray,
And, 'twixt life and death, was snatch'd away
    To the joyless Elfin bower.

"But wist I of a woman bold,
    Who thrice my brow durst sign,
I might regain my mortal mold,
    As fair a form as thine." —   360

She cross'd him once — she cross'd him twice —
   That lady was so brave;
The fouler grew his goblin hue,
   The darker grew the cave.

She cross'd him thrice, that lady bold;
   He rose beneath her hand
The fairest knight on Scottish mold,
   Her brother, Ethert Brand!

Merry it is in good greenwood,
   When the mavis and merle are singing,   370
But merrier were they in Dunfermline gray,
   When all the bells were ringing.

XVI.

Just as the minstrel sounds were staid,
A stranger climb'd the steepy glade;
His martial step, his stately mien,
His hunting suit of Lincoln green,
His eagle glance, remembrance claims —
'Tis Snowdoun's Knight, 'tis James Fitz-James.
Ellen beheld as in a dream,
Then, starting, scarce suppress'd a scream: 380
"O stranger! in such hour of fear,
What evil hap has brought thee here?"
"An evil hap how can it be,

That bids me look again on thee?
By promise bound, my former guide
Met me betimes this morning tide,
And marshall'd, over bank and bourne,
The happy path of my return." —
"The happy path! — what! said he nought
Of war, of battle to be fought, 390
Of guarded pass?" — "No, by my faith!
Nor saw I aught could augur scathe." —
"O haste thee, Allan, to the kern:
Yonder his tartans I discern;
Learn thou his purpose, and conjure
That he will guide the stranger sure! —
What prompted thee, unhappy man?
The meanest serf in Roderick's clan
Had not been bribed by love or fear,
Unknown to him, to guide thee here." — 400

XVII.

"Sweet Ellen, dear my life must be,
Since it is worthy care from thee;
Yet life I hold but idle breath,
When love or honor's weigh'd with death.
Then let me profit by my chance,
And speak my purpose bold at once.
I come to bear thee from a wild

Where ne'er before such blossom smiled;
By this soft hand to lead thee far
From frantic scenes of feud and war.   410
Near Bochastle my horses wait;
They bear us soon to Stirling gate.
I'll place thee in a lovely bower,
I'll guard thee like a tender flower" —
"O! hush, Sir Knight! 'twere female art,
To say I do not read thy heart;
Too much, before, my selfish ear
Was idly soothed my praise to hear.
That fatal bait hath lured thee back,
In deathful hour, o'er dangerous track;   420
And how, O how, can I atone
The wreck my vanity brought on! —
One way remains — I'll tell him all —
Yes! struggling bosom, forth it shall!
Thou, whose light folly bears the blame,
Buy thine own pardon with thy shame!
But first — my father is a man
Outlaw'd and exil'd, under ban;
The price of blood is on his head,
With me 'twere infamy to wed.   430
Still would'st thou speak? — then hear the truth!
Fitz-James, there is a noble youth —
If yet he is! — exposed for me
And mine to dread extremity —

Thou hast the secret of my heart;
Forgive, be generous, and depart!"

XVIII.

Fitz-James knew every wily train
A lady's fickle heart to gain,
But here he knew and felt them vain.
There shot no glance from Ellen's eye, 440
To give her steadfast speech the lie;
In maiden confidence she stood,
Though mantled in her cheek the blood,
And told her love with such a sigh
Of deep and hopeless agony,
As death had seal'd her Malcolm's doom,
And she sat sorrowing on his tomb.
Hope vanish'd from Fitz-James's eye,
But not with hope fled sympathy.
He proffer'd to attend her side, 450
As brother would a sister guide. —
" O! little know'st thou Roderick's heart!
Safer for both we go apart.
O haste thee, and from Allan learn,
If thou may'st trust yon wily kern."
With hand upon his forehead laid,
The conflict of his mind to shade,
A parting step or two he made;

Then, as some thought had cross'd his brain,
He paus'd, and turn'd, and came again.   460

XIX.

"Hear, lady, yet, a parting word! —
It chanced in fight that my poor sword
Preserved the life of Scotland's lord.
This ring the grateful Monarch gave,
And bade, when I had boon to crave,
To bring it back, and boldly claim
The recompense that I would name.
Ellen, I am no courtly lord,
But one who lives by lance and sword,
Whose castle is his helm and shield,   470
His lordship, the embattled field.
What from a prince can I demand,
Who neither reck of state nor land?
Ellen, thy hand — the ring is thine;
Each guard and usher knows the sign.
Seek thou the king without delay;
This signet shall secure thy way;
And claim thy suit, whate'er it be,
As ransom of his pledge to me." —
He placed the golden circlet on,   480
Paused — kiss'd her hand — and then was gone.
The aged Minstrel stood aghast,
So hastily Fitz-James shot past.

He join'd his guide, and wending down
The ridges of the mountain brown,
Across the stream they took their way,
That joins Loch Katrine to Achray.

XX.

All in the Trosachs' glen was still,
Noontide was sleeping on the hill:
Sudden his guide whoop'd loud and high —   490
" Murdoch ! was that a signal cry ? " —
He stammer'd forth, — "I shout to scare
You raven from his dainty fare."
He look'd — he knew the raven's prey,
His own brave steed : — " Ah ! gallant gray !
For thee — for me, perchance — 'twere well
We ne'er had seen the Trosachs' dell. —
Murdoch, move first — but silently;
Whistle or whoop, and thou shalt die ! " —
Jealous and sullen on they fared,   500
Each silent, each upon his guard.

XXI.

Now wound the path its dizzy ledge
Around a precipice's edge,
When lo ! a wasted female form,
Blighted by wrath of sun and storm,
In tatter'd weeds and wild array,

Stood on a cliff beside the way,
And glancing round her restless eye,
Upon the wood, the rock, the sky,
Seem'd nought to mark, yet all to spy. 510
Her brow was wreath'd with gaudy broom;
With gesture wild she waved a plume
Of feathers, which the eagles fling
To crag and cliff from dusky wing;
Such spoils her desperate step had sought,
Where scarce was footing for the goat.
The tartan plaid she first descried,
And shriek'd till all the rocks replied;
As loud she laugh'd when near they drew,
For then the Lowland garb she knew; 520
And then her hands she wildly wrung,
And then she wept, and then she sung. —
She sung! — the voice, in better time,
Perchance to harp or lute might chime;
And now, though strain'd and roughen'd, still
Rung wildly sweet to dale and hill.

XXII.

Song.

They bid me sleep, they bid me pray,
   They say my brain is warp'd and wrung —
I cannot sleep on Highland brae,
   I cannot pray in Highland tongue. 530

THE PROPHECY.

But were I now where Allan glides,
Or heard my native Devan's tides,
So sweetly would I rest, and pray
That Heaven would close my wintry day!

'Twas thus my hair they bade me braid,
   They made me to the church repair;
It was my bridal morn they said,
   And my true love would meet me there.
But woe betide the cruel guile,
That drown'd in blood the morning smile!   540
And woe betide the fairy dream!
I only waked to sob and scream. —

XXIII.

"Who is this maid? what means her lay?
She hovers o'er the hollow way,
And flutters wide her mantle gray,
As the lone heron spreads his wing,
By twilight, o'er a haunted spring." —
"'Tis Blanche of Devan," Murdoch said,
"A crazed and captive Lowland maid,
Ta'en on the morn she was a bride,   550
When Roderick foray'd Devan-side.
The gay bridegroom resistance made,
And felt our Chief's unconquer'd blade.

I marvel she is now at large,
But oft she 'scapes from Maudlin's charge. —
Hence, brain-sick fool!" — He raised his bow : —
"Now, if thou strik'st her but one blow,
I'll pitch thee from the cliff as far
As ever peasant pitch'd a bar!" —
"Thanks, champion, thanks!" the Maniac cried,
And press'd her to Fitz-James's side   561
"See the gray pennons I prepare,
To seek my true-love through the air!
I will not lend that savage groom,
To break his fall, one downy plume!
No! — deep amid disjointed stones,
The wolves shall batten on his bones,
And then shall his detested plaid,
By bush and brier in mid air staid,
Wave forth a banner fair and free,   570
Meet signal for their revelry." —

XXIV.

"Hush thee, poor maiden, and be still!" —
"O! thou look'st kindly, and I will. —
Mine eye has dried and wasted been,
But still it loves the Lincoln green;
And, though mine ear is all unstrung,
Still, still it loves the Lowland tongue.

"For O my sweet William was forester true,
  He stole poor Blanche's heart away!
His coat it was all of the greenwood hue,   580
  And so blithely he trill'd the Lowland lay!
"It was not that I meant to tell . . .
But thou art wise, and guessest well."
Then, in a low and broken tone,
And hurried note, the song went on.
Still on the clansman, fearfully,
She fix'd her apprehensive eye;
Then turn'd it on the Knight, and then
Her look glanced wildly o'er the glen.

XXV.

"The toils are pitch'd, and the stakes are set,   590
  Ever sing merrily, merrily;
The bows they bend, and the knives they whet,
  Hunters live so cheerily.

"It was a stag, a stag of ten,
  Bearing its branches sturdily;
He came stately down the glen,
  Ever sing hardily, hardily.

"It was there he met with a wounded doe,
  She was bleeding deathfully;
She warn'd him of the toils below,   600
  O so faithfully, faithfully!

"He had an eye, and he could heed,
  Ever sing warily, warily;
He had a foot, and he could speed —
  Hunters watch so narrowly." —

XXVI.

Fitz-James's mind was passiod-toss'd,
When Ellen's hints and fears were lost;
But Murdoch's shout suspicion wrought,
And Blanche's song conviction brought.
Not like a stag that spies the snare, 610
But lion of the hunt aware,
He waved at once his blade on high,
"Disclose thy treachery, or die!" —
Forth at full speed the Clansman flew,
But in his race his bow he drew.
The shaft just grazed Fitz-James's crest,
And thrill'd in Blanche's faded breast. —
Murdoch of Alpine! prove thy speed,
For ne'er had Alpine's son such need;
With heart of fire, and foot of wind, 620
The fierce avenger is behind!
Fate judges of the rapid strife
The forfeit death — the prize is life;
Thy kindred ambush lies before,
Close couch'd upon the heathery moor;
Them couldst thou reach! — it may not be —

Thine ambush'd kin thou ne'er shalt see,
The fiery Saxon gains on thee! —
Resistless speeds the deadly thrust,
As lightning strikes the pine to dust;   630
With foot and hand Fitz-James must strain
Ere he can win his blade again.
Bent o'er the fall'n, with falcon eye,
He grimly smiled to see him die;
Then slower wended back his way,
Where the poor maiden bleeding lay.

XXVII.

She sate beneath the birchen tree,
Her elbow resting on her knee;
She had withdrawn the fatal shaft,
And gazed on it, and feebly laugh'd;   640
Her wreath of broom and feathers gray
Daggled with blood, beside her lay.
The Knight to stanch the life-stream tried, —
"Stranger, it is in vain!" she cried.
"This hour of death has given me more
Of reason's power than years before;
For, as these ebbing veins decay,
My frenzied visions fade away.
A helpless injured wretch I die,
And something tells me in thine eye,   650
That thou wert mine avenger born. —

Seest thou this tress? — O! still I've worn
This little tress of yellow hair,
Through danger, frenzy, and despair!
It once was bright and clear as thine,
But blood and tears have dimm'd its shine.
I will not tell thee when 'twas shred,
Nor from what guiltless victim's head —
My brain would turn! — but it shall wave
Like plumage on thy helmet brave,   660
Till sun and wind shall bleach the stain,
  And thou wilt bring it me again. —
I waver still. — O God! more bright
Let reason beam her parting light! —
O! by thy knighthood's honored sign,
And for thy life preserved by mine,
When thou shalt see a darksome man,
Who boasts him Chief of Alpine's Clan,
With tartans broad and shadowy plume,
And hand of blood, and brow of gloom,   670
Be thy heart bold, thy weapon strong,
And wreak poor Blanche of Devan's wrong! —
They watch for thee by pass and fell . . .
Avoid the path . . . O God! . . . farewell." —

XXVIII.

A kindly heart had brave Fitz-James;
Fast pour'd his eyes at pity's claims,

And now, with mingled grief and ire,
He saw the murder'd maid expire.
"God, in my need, be my relief,
As I wreak this on yonder Chief!"   680
A lock from Blanche's tresses fair
He blended with her bridegroom's hair;
The mingled braid in blood he dyed,
And placed it on his bonnet-side:
"By Him whose word is truth, I swear,
No other favor will I wear,
Till this sad token I imbrue
In the best blood of Roderick Dhu! —
But hark! what means yon faint halloo?
The chase is up, — but they shall know,   690
The stag at bay's a dangerous foe."
Barr'd from the known but guarded way,
Through copse and cliffs Fitz-James must stray,
And oft must change his desperate track,
By stream and precipice turn'd back.
Heartless, fatigued, and faint, at length,
From lack of food and loss of strength,
He couch'd him in a thicket hoar,
And thought his toils and perils o'er: —
"Of all my rash adventures past,   700
This frantic feat must prove the last!
Who e'er so mad but might have guess'd,
That all this Highland hornet's nest

Would muster up in swarms as soon
As e'er they heard of bands at Doune? —
Like bloodhounds now they search me out, —
Hark, to the whistle and the shout! —
If further through the wilds I go,
I only fall upon the foe:
I'll couch me here till evening gray,   710
Then darkling try my dangerous way."

XXIX.

The shades of eve come slowly down,
The woods are wrapp'd in deeper brown,
The owl awakens from her dell,
The fox is heard upon the fell;
Enough remains of glimmering light
To guide the wanderer's steps aright,
Yet not enough from far to show
His figure to the watchful foe.
With cautious step, and ear awake,   720
He climbs the crag and threads the brake;
And not the summer solstice, there,
Temper'd the m'dnight mountain air,
But every breeze that swept the wold
Benumb'd his drenched limbs with cold.
In dread, in danger, and alone,
Famish'd and chill'd, through ways unknown,
Tangled and steep, he journey'd on;

Till, as a rock's huge point he turn'd,
A watch-fire close before him burn'd. 730

XXX.

Beside its embers red and clear,
Bask'd, in his plaid, a mountaineer;
And up he sprang with sword in hand, —
"Thy name and purpose! Saxon, stand!"
"A stranger." — "What dost thou require?" —
"Rest and a guide, and food and fire.
My life's beset, my path is lost,
The gale has chill'd my limbs with frost."
"Art thou a friend to Roderick?" — "No." —
"Thou darest not call thyself a foe?" — 740
"I dare! to him and all the band
"He brings to aid his murderous hand."
"Bold words! — but, though the beast of game
The privilege of chase may claim,
Though space and law the stag we lend,
Ere hound we slip, or bow we bend,
Who ever reck'd, where, how, or when,
The prowling fox was trapp'd or slain?
Thus treacherous scouts, — yet sure they lie,
Who say thou cam'st a secret spy!" — 750
"They do, by heaven! — Come Roderick Dhu,
And of his clan the boldest two,
And let me but till morning rest,

I write the falsehood on their crest." —
"If by the blaze I mark aright,
Thou bear'st the belt and spur of Knight."
"Then by these tokens may'st thou know
Each proud oppressor's mortal foe." —
"Enough, enough ; sit down, and share
A soldier's couch, a soldier's fare."   760

XXXI.

He gave him of his Highland cheer,
The harden'd flesh of mountain deer ;
Dry fuel on the fire he laid,
And bade the Saxon share his plaid.
He tended him like welcome guest,
Then thus his further speech address'd : —
" Stranger, I am to Roderick Dhu
A clansman born, a kinsman true ;
Each word against his honor spoke,
Demands of me avenging stroke ;   770
Yet more, — upon thy fate, 'tis said,
A mighty augury is laid.
It rests with me to wind my horn, —
Thou art with numbers overborne ;
It rests with me, here, brand to brand,
Worn as thou art, to bid thee stand :
But, not for clan, nor kindred's cause,
Will I depart from honor's laws ;

THE PROPHECY.

To assail a wearied man were shame,
And stranger is a holy name; 780
Guidance and rest, and food and fire,
In vain he never must require.
Then rest thee here till dawn of day;
Myself will guide thee on the way,
O'er stock and stone, through watch and ward,
Till past Clan-Alpine's outmost guard,
As far as Coilantogle's ford;
From thence thy warrant is thy sword." —
" I take thy courtesy, by heaven,
As freely as 'tis nobly given!" — 790
" Well, rest thee; for the bittern's cry
Sings us the lake's wild lullaby." —
With that he shook the gather'd heath,
And spread his plaid upon the wreath;
And the brave foemen, side by side,
Lay peaceful down like brothers tried,
And slept until the dawning beam
Purpled the mountain and the stream.

CANTO FIFTH.

The Combat.

I.

Fair as the earliest beam of eastern light,
  When first, by the bewilder'd pilgrim spied,
It smiles upon the dreary brow of night,
  And silvers o'er the torrent's foaming tide,
And lights the fearful path on mountain side;—
  Fair as that beam, although the fairest far,
Giving to horror grace, to danger pride,
  Shine martial Faith, and Courtesy's bright star,
Through all the wreckful storms that cloud the brow
    of War.

II.

That early beam, so fair and sheen, 10
Was twinkling through the hazel screen,
When, rousing at its glimmer red,
The warriors left their lowly bed,
Look'd out upon the dappled sky,
Mutter'd their soldier matins by,
And then awaked their fire, to steal,
As short and rude, their soldier meal.

That o'er, the Gael around him threw
His graceful plaid of varied hue,
And, true to promise, led the way,
By thicket green and mountain gray.
A wildering path! — they winded now
Along the precipice's brow,
Commanding the rich scenes beneath,
The windings of the Forth and Teith,
And all the vales between that lie,
Till Stirling's turrets melt in sky;
Then, sunk in copse, their farthest glance
Gain'd not the length of horseman's lance.
'Twas oft so steep, the foot was fain
Assistance from the hand to gain;
So tangled oft, that, bursting through,
Each hawthorn shed her showers of dew, —
That diamond dew, so pure and clear,
It rivals all but Beauty's tear

III.

At length they came where, stern and steep,
The hill sinks down upon the deep.
Here Vennachar in silver flows,
There, ridge on ridge, Benledi rose;
Ever the hollow path twined on,
Beneath steep bank and threatening stone;
An hundred men might hold the post,

With hardihood, against a host.
The rugged mountain's scanty cloak
Was dwarfish shrubs of birch and oak,
With shingles bare, and cliffs between,
And patches bright of bracken green,
And heather black, that waved so high,
It held the copse in rivalry.
But where the lake slept deep and still,   50
Dank osiers fringed the swamp and hill
And oft both path and hill were torn,
Where wintry torrents down had borne,
And heap'd upon the cumber'd land
Its wreck of gravel, rocks, and sand.
So toilsome was the road to trace,
The guide, abating of his pace,
Led slowly through the pass's jaws,
And ask'd Fitz-James by what strange cause
He sought these wilds, traversed by few,   60
Without a pass from Roderick Dhu.

IV.

"Brave Gael, my pass, in danger tried,
Hangs in my belt, and by my side;
Yet, sooth to tell," the Saxon said,
"I dream'd not now to claim its aid.
When here, but three days since, I came,
Bewilder'd in pursuit of game,

All seem'd as peaceful and as still,
As the mist slumbering on yon hill;
Thy dangerous Chief was then afar,
Nor soon expected back from war.
Thus said, at least, my mountain-guide,
Though deep, perchance, the villain lied."
" Yet why a second venture try ? " —
" A warrior thou, and ask me why ! —
Moves our free course by such fix'd cause,
As gives the poor mechanic laws ?
Enough, I sought to drive away
The lazy hours of peaceful day;
Slight cause will then suffice to guide
A Knight's free footsteps far and wide, —
A falcon flown, a greyhound stray'd,
The merry glance of mountain maid:
Or, if a path be dangerous known,
The danger's self is lure alone." —

V.

" Thy secret keep, I urge thee not; —
Yet, ere again ye sought this spot,
Say, heard ye naught of Lowland war,
Against Clan-Alpine rais'd by Mar ? " —
" No, by my words; — of bands prepared
To guard King James's sports I heard;
Nor doubt I aught, but, when they hear

This muster of the mountaineer,
Their pennons will abroad be flung,
Which else in Doune had peaceful hung." —
"Free be they flung! for we were loth
Their silken folds should feast the moth.
Free be they flung! — as free shall wave
Clan-Alpine's pine in banner brave.
But, Stranger, peaceful since you came,   100
Bewilder'd in the mountain game,
Whence the bold boast by which you show
Vich-Alpine's vow'd and mortal foe?" —
"Warrior, but yester-morn, I knew
Naught of thy Chieftain, Roderick Dhu,
Save as an outlaw'd desperate man,
The chief of a rebellious clan,
Who, in the Regent's court and sight,
With ruffian dagger stabb'd a knight:
Yet this alone might from his part   110
Sever each true and loyal heart." —

VI.

Wrathful at such arraignment foul,
Dark lower'd the clansman's sable scowl.
A space he paused, then sternly said,
"And heard'st thou why he drew his blade?
Heard'st thou that shameful word and blow

Brought Roderick's vengeance on his foe?
What reck'd the Chieftain if he stood
On Highland heath or Holy-Rood?
He rights such wrong where it is given, 120
If it were in the court of heaven." —
" Still was it outrage; — yet, 'tis true,
Not then claim'd sovereignty his due;
While Albany, with feeble hand,
Held borrow'd truncheon of command,
The young King, mew'd in Stirling tower,
Was stranger to respect and power.
But then, thy Chieftain's robber life! —
Winning mean prey by causeless strife,
Wrenching from ruin'd Lowland swain 130
His herds and harvest rear'd in vain, —
Methinks a soul like thine should scorn
The spoils from such foul foray borne." —

VII.

The Gael beheld him grim the while,
And answer'd with disdainful smile, —
" Saxon, from yonder mountain high,
I mark'd thee send delighted eye,
Far to the south and east, where lay,
Extended in succession gay,
Deep waving fields and pastures green, 140

With gentle slopes and groves between : —
These fertile plains, that soften'd vale,
Were once the birthright of the Gael;
The stranger came with iron hand,
And from our fathers reft the land.
Where dwell we now! See, rudely swell
Crag over crag, and fell o'er fell.
Ask we this savage hill we tread
For fatten'd steer or household bread;
Ask we for flocks these shingles dry,   150
And well the mountain might reply, —
'To you, as to your sires of yore,
Belong the target and claymore!
I give you shelter in my breast,
Your own good blades must win the rest.'
Pent in this fortress of the North,
Think'st thou we will not sally forth,
To spoil the spoiler as we may,
And from the robber rend the prey?
Ay, by my soul! — While on yon plain   160
The Saxon rears one shock of grain;
While, of ten thousand herds, there strays
But one along yon river's maze, —
The Gael, of plain and river heir,
Shall, with strong hand, redeem his share.
Where live the mountain Chiefs who hold
That plundering Lowland field and fold

Is aught but retribution true?
Seek other cause 'gainst Roderick Dhu."

VIII.

Answer'd Fitz-James, — "And, if I sought,   170
Think'st thou no other could be brought?
What deem ye of my path waylaid?
My life given o'er to ambuscade?"
"As of a meed to rashness due:
Hadst thou sent warning fair and true, —
I seek my hound, or falcon stray'd,
I seek, good faith, a Highland maid, —
Free hadst thou been to come and go;
But secret path marks secret foe.
Nor yet, for this, even as a spy,   180
Hadst thou, unheard, been doom'd to die,
Save to fulfil an augury." —
"Well, let it pass; nor will I now
Fresh cause of enmity avow,
To chafe thy mood and cloud thy brow.
Enough, I am by promise tied
To match me with this man of pride:
Twice have I sought Clan-Alpine's glen
In peace; but when I come again,
I come with banner, brand, and bow,   190
As leader seeks his mortal foe.
For love-lorn swain, in lady's bower,

Ne'er panted for the appointed hour,
As I, until before me stand
This rebel Chieftain and his band!" —

IX.

"Have, then, thy wish!" — He whistled shrill,
And he was answer'd from the hill;
Wild as the scream of the curlew,
From crag to crag the signal-flew.
Instant, through copse and heath, arose   200
Bonnets and spears and bended bows;
On right, on left, above, below,
Sprung up at once the lurking foe;
From shingles gray their lances start,
The bracken bush sends forth the dart,
The rushes and the willow-wand
Are bristling into axe and brand,
And every tuft of broom gives life
To plaided warrior arm'd for strife.
That whistle garrison'd the glen   210
At once with full five hundred men,
As if the yawning hill to heaven
A subterranean host had given.
Watching their leader's beck and will,
All silent there they stood, and still.
Like the loose crags, whose threatening mass
Lay tottering o'er the hollow pass,

As if an infant's touch could urge
Their headlong passage down the verge,
With step and weapon forward flung,   220
Upon the mountain-side they hung.
The mountaineer cast glance of pride
Along Benledi's living side,
Then fix'd his eye and sable brow
Full on Fitz-James — "How say'st thou now?
These are Clan-Alpine's warriors true;
And, Saxon, — I am Roderick Dhu!"

X.

Fitz-James was brave: — Though to his heart
The life-blood thrill'd with sudden start,
He mann'd himself with dauntless air,   230
Return'd the Chief his haughty stare,
His back against a rock he bore,
And firmly placed his foot before: —
"Come one, come all! this rock shall fly
From its firm base as soon as I." —
Sir Roderick mark'd — and in his eyes
Respect was mingled with surprise,
And the stern joy which warriors feel
In foemen worthy of their steel.
Short space he stood — then waved his hand: 240
Down sunk the disappearing band;
Each warrior vanish'd where he stood,

In broom or bracken, heath or wood;
Sunk brand and spear and bended bow,
In osiers pale and copses low;
It seem'd as if their mother Earth
Had swallow'd up her warlike birth.
The wind's last breath had toss'd in air,
Pennon, and plaid, and plumage fair, —
The next but swept a lone hill-side,   250
Where heath and fern were waving wide:
The sun's last glance was glinted back,
From spear and glaive, from targe and jack, —
The next, all unreflected, shone
On bracken green and cold gray stone.

XI.

Fitz-James look'd round, — yet scarce believed
The witness that his sight received;
Such apparition well might seem
Delusion of a dreadful dream.
Sir Roderick in suspense he eyed,   260
And to his look the Chief replied,
" Fear naught — nay, that I need not say —
But — doubt not aught from mine array.
Thou art my guest; — I pledged my word
As far as Coilantogle ford:
Nor would I call a clansman's brand

For aid against one valiant hand,
Though on our strife lay every vale
Rent by the Saxon from the Gael.
So move we on; — I only meant   270
To show the reed on which you leant,
Deeming this path you might pursue
Without a pass from Roderick Dhu." —
They moved: — I said Fitz-James was brave,
As ever knight that belted glaive;
Yet dare not say, that now his blood
Kept on its wont and temper'd flood,
As, following Roderick's stride, he drew
That seeming lonesome pathway through,
Which yet, by fearful proof, was rife   280
With lances, that to take his life
Waited but signal from a guide,
So late dishonor'd and defied.
Ever, by stealth, his eye sought round
The vanish'd guardians of the ground,
And still, from copse and heather deep,
Fancy saw spear and broadsword peep,
And in the plover's shrilly strain,
The signal whistle heard again.
Nor breathed he free till far behind   290
The pass was left; for then they wind
Along a wide and level green,
Where neither tree nor tuft was seen,

Nor rush nor bush of broom was near,
To hide a bonnet or a spear.

XII.

The Chief in silence strode before,
And reach'd that torrent's sounding shore,
Which, daughter of three mighty lakes,
From Vennachar in silver breaks,
Sweeps through the plain, and ceaseless mines 300
On Bochastle the mouldering lines,
Where Rome, the Empress of the world,
Of yore her eagle wings unfurl'd.
And here his course the Chieftain staid,
Threw down his target and his plaid,
And to the Lowland warrior said : —
" Bold Saxon ! to his promise just,
Vich-Alpine has discharged his trust.
This murderous Chief, this ruthless man,
This head of a rebellious clan, 310
Hath led thee safe, through watch and ward,
Far past Clan-Alpine's outmost guard.
Now, man to man, and steel to steel,
A Chieftain's vengeance thou shalt feel.
See, here, all vantageless, I stand,
Arm'd, like thyself, with single brand :
For this is Coilantogle ford,
And thou must keep thee with thy sword."

XIII.

The Saxon paused: — "I ne'er delay'd,
When foeman bade me draw my blade ; 320
Nay more, brave Chief, I vow'd thy death :
Yet sure thy fair and generous faith,
And my deep debt for life preserved,
A better meed have well deserved : —
Can naught but blood our feud atone ?
Are there no means ?" — "No, Stranger, none !
And hear, — to fire thy flagging zeal, —
The Saxon cause rests on thy steel ;
For thus spoke Fate, by prophet bred
Between the living and the dead : 330
' Who spills the foremost foeman's life,
His party conquers in the strife.' "
"Then, by my word," the Saxon said,
"The riddle is already read.
Seek yonder brake beneath the cliff, —
There lies Red Murdoch, stark and stiff.
Thus Fate hath solved her prophecy,
Then yield to Fate, and not to me.
To James, at Stirling, let us go,
When, if thou wilt be still his foe, 340
Or if the King shall not agree
To grant thee grace and favor free,
I plight mine honor, oath, and word,
That, to thy native strengths restored,

With each advantage shalt thou stand,
That aids thee now to guard thy land." —

XIV.

Dark lightning flash'd from Roderick's eye:
" Soars thy presumption, then, so high,
Because a wretched kern ye slew,
Homage to name to Roderick Dhu?   350
He yields not, he, to man nor Fate!
Thou add'st but fuel to my hate: —
My clansman's blood demands revenge. —
Not yet prepared? — By heaven, I change
My thought, and hold thy valor light
As that of some vain carpet-knight,
Who ill deserved my courteous care,
And whose best boast is but to wear
A braid of his fair lady's hair." —
" I thank thee, Roderick, for the word!   360
It nerves my heart, it steels my sword;
For I have sworn this braid to stain
In the best blood that warms thy vein.
Now, truce, farewell! and, ruth, begone! —
Yet think not that by thee alone,
Proud Chief! can courtesy be shown;
Though not from copse, or heath, or cairn,
Start at my whistle clansmen stern,
Of this small horn one feeble blast

THE COMBAT.

Would fearful odds against thee cast. 370
But fear not — doubt not — which thou wilt —
We try this quarrel hilt to hilt." —
Then each at once his falchion drew,
Each on the ground his scabbard threw,
Each look'd to sun, and stream, and plain,
As what they ne'er might see again;
Then foot and point and eye opposed,
In dubious strife they darkly closed.

XV.

Ill fared it then with Roderick Dhu,
That on the field his targe he threw, 380
Whose brazen studs and tough bull-hide
Had death so often dash'd aside;
For, train'd abroad his arms to wield,
Fitz-James's blade was sword and shield.
He practised every pass and ward,
To thrust, to strike, to feint, to guard;
While less expert, though stronger far,
The Gael maintain'd unequal war.
Three times in closing strife they stood,
And thrice the Saxon blade drank blood; 390
No stinted draught, no scanty tide,
The gushing flood the tartans dyed.
Fierce Roderick felt the fatal drain,
And shower'd his blows like wintry rain;

And, as firm rock, or castle roof,
Against the winter shower is proof,
The foe, invulnerable still,
Foil'd his wild rage by steady skill;
Till, at advantage ta'en, his brand
Forced Roderick's weapon from his hand,   400
And, backward borne upon the lea,
Brought the proud Chieftain to his knee.

XVI.

"Now, yield thee, or, by Him who made
The world, thy heart's blood dyes my blade!" —
"Thy threats, thy mercy, I defy!
Let recreant yield, who fears to die."
Like adder darting from his coil,
Like wolf that dashes through the toil,
Like mountain-cat who guards her young,
Full at Fitz-James's throat he sprung;   410
Receiv'd, but reck'd not of a wound,
And lock'd his arms his foeman round. —
Now, gallant Saxon, hold thine own!
No maiden's hand is round thee thrown!
That desperate grasp thy frame might feel,
Through bars of brass and triple steel!
They tug, they strain! down, down they go,
The Gael above, Fitz-James below.

The Chieftain's gripe his throat compress'd,
His knee was planted on his breast;
His clotted locks he backward threw,
Across his brow his hand he drew,
From blood and mist to clear his sight,
Then gleam'd aloft his dagger bright! —
But hate and fury ill supplied
The stream of life's exhausted tide,
And all too late the advantage came,
To turn the odds of deadly game;
For, while the dagger gleam'd on high,
Reel'd soul and sense, reel'd brain and eye.
Down came the blow! but in the heath
The erring blade found bloodless sheath.
The struggling foe may now unclasp
The fainting Chief's relaxing grasp;
Unwounded from the dreadful close,
But breathless all, Fitz-James arose.

XVII.

He falter'd thanks to Heaven for life,
Redeem'd, unhoped, from desperate strife;
Next on his foe his look he cast,
Whose every gasp appear'd his last;
In Roderick's gore he dipp'd the braid, —
" Poor Blanche! thy wrongs are dearly paid:

Yet with thy foe must die, or live,
The praise that Faith and Valor give."
With that he blew a bugle note,
Undid the collar from his throat,
Unbonneted, and by the wave
Sate down his brow and hands to lave.
Then faint afar are heard the feet
Of rushing steeds in gallop fleet; 450
The sounds increase, and now are seen
Four mounted squires in Lincoln green;
Two who bear lance, and two who lead,
By loosen'd rein, a saddled steed;
Each onward held his headlong course,
And by Fitz-James rein'd up his horse, —
With wonder view'd the bloody spot —
"Exclaim not, gallants! question not. —
You, Herbert and Luffness, alight,
And bind the wounds of yonder knight; 460
Let the gray palfrey bear his weight,
We destined for a fairer freight,
And bring him on to Stirling straight;
I will before at better speed,
To seek fresh horse and fitting weed.
The sun rides high; — I must be boune,
To see the archer-game at noon;
But lightly Bayard clears the lea. —
De Vaux and Herries, follow me.

XVIII.

"Stand, Bayard, stand!" — the steed obey'd 470
With arching neck and bended head,
And glancing eye, and quivering ear,
As if he loved his lord to hear.
No foot Fitz-James in stirrup staid,
No grasp upon the saddle laid,
But wreath'd his left hand in the mane,
And lightly bounded from the plain,
Turn'd on the horse his armed heel,
And stirr'd his courage with the steel.
Bounded the fiery steed in air, 480
The rider sate erect and fair,
Then, like a bolt from steel cross-bow
Forth launch'd, along the plain they go.
They dash'd that rapid torrent through,
And up Carhonie's hill they flew;
Still at the gallop prick'd the Knight,
His merry-men follow'd as they might,
Along thy banks, swift Teith! they ride,
And in the race they mock thy tide;
Torry and Lendrick now are past, 490
And Deanstown lies behind them cast;
They rise, the banner'd towers of Doune,
They sink in distant woodland soon;
Blair-Drummond sees the hoofs strike fire,
They sweep like breeze through Ochtertyre;

They mark just glance and disappear
The lofty brow of ancient Kier;
They bathe their coursers' sweltering sides,
Dark Forth! amid thy sluggish tides,
And on the opposing shore take ground, 500
With plash, with scramble, and with bound.
Right-hand they leave thy cliffs, Craig-Forth!
And soon the bulwark of the North,
Gray Stirling, with her towers and town,
Upon their fleet career look'd down.

XIX.

As up the flinty path they strain'd,
Sudden his steed the leader rein'd;
A signal to his squire he flung,
Who instant to his stirrup sprung: —
"Seest thou, De Vaux, yon woodsman gray, 510
Who town-ward holds the rocky way,
Of stature tall and poor array?
Mark'st thou the firm, yet active stride,
With which he scales the mountain side?
Know'st thou from whence he comes, or whom?"
"No, by my word; — a burly groom
He seems, who in the field or chase
A baron's train would nobly grace." —
"Out, out, De Vaux! can fear supply,
And jealousy, no sharper eye? 520

Afar, ere to the hill he drew,
That stately form and step I knew;
Like form in Scotland is not seen,
Treads not such step on Scottish green.
'Tis James of Douglas, by St. Serle!
The uncle of the banish'd Earl.
Away, away, to court, to show
The near approach of dreaded foe:
The King must stand upon his guard;
Douglas and he must meet prepared."   530
Then right-hand wheel'd their steeds, and straight
They won the castle's postern gate.

XX.

The Douglas, who had bent his way
From Cambus-Kenneth's abbey gray,
Now, as he climb'd the rocky shelf,
Held sad communion with himself: —
"Yes! all is true my fears could frame;
A prisoner lies the noble Græme,
And fiery Roderick soon will feel
The vengeance of the royal steel.   540
I, only I, can ward their fate, —
God grant the ransom come not late!
The abbess hath her promise given,
My child shall be the bride of heaven; —
— Be pardon'd one repining tear!

For He, who gave her, knows how dear,
How excellent! — but that is by,
And now my busines is — to die.
— Ye towers! within whose circuit dread
A Douglas by his sovereign bled; 550
And thou, O sad and fatal mound!
That oft hast heard the death-axe sound,
As on the noblest of the land
Fell the stern headsman's bloody hand, —
The dungeon, block, and nameless tomb
Prepare, — for Douglas seeks his doom!
But hark! what blithe and jolly peal
Makes the Franciscan steeple reel?
And see! upon the crowded street,
In motley groups what masquers meet! 560
Banner and pageant, pipe and drum,
And merry morrice-dancers come.
I guess, by all this quaint array,
The burghers hold their sports to-day.
James will be there; he loves such show,
Where the good yeoman bends his bow,
And the tough wrestler foils his foe,
As well as where, in proud career,
The high-born tilter shivers spear.
I'll follow to the Castle-park, 570
And play my prize; — King James shall mark,
If age has tamed these sinews stark,

Whose force so oft, in happier days,
His boyish wonder loved to praise."

XXI.

The Castle gates were open flung,
The quivering draw-bridge rock'd and rung,
And echo'd loud the flinty street
Beneath the coursers' clattering feet,
As slowly down the steep descent
Fair Scotland's King and nobles went, 580
While all along the crowded way
Was jubilee and loud huzza.
And ever James was bending low,
To his white jennet's saddlebow,
Doffing his cap to city dame,
Who smiled and blush'd for pride and shame.
And well the simperer might be vain, —
He chose the fairest of the train.
Gravely he greets each city sire,
Commends each pageant's quaint attire, 590
Gives to the dancers thanks aloud,
And smiles and nods upon the crowd,
Who rend the heavens with their acclaims,
"Long live the Commons' King, King James!"
Behind the King throng'd peer and knight,
And noble dame and damsel bright,
Whose fiery steeds ill brook'd the stay

Of the steep street and crowded way.
— But in the train you might discern
Dark lowering brow and visage stern; 600
There nobles mourn'd their pride restrain'd,
And the mean burgher's joys disdain'd;
And chiefs, who, hostage for their clan,
Were each from home a banish'd man,
There thought upon their own gray tower,
Their waving woods, their feudal power,
And deem'd themselves a shameful part
Of pageant which they cursed in heart.

XXII.

Now, in the Castle-park, drew out
Their chequer'd bands the joyous rout. 610
There morricers, with bell at heel,
And blade in hand, their mazes wheel;
But chief, beside the butts, there stand
Bold Robin Hood and all his band, —
Friar Tuck with quarterstaff and cowl,
Old Scathelocke with his surly scowl,
Maid Marion, fair as ivory bone,
Scarlet, and Mutch, and Little John;
Their bugles challenge all that will,
In archery to prove their skill. 620
The Douglas bent a bow of might, —
His first shaft center'd in the white,

And when in turn he shot again,
His second split the first in twain.
From the King's hand must Douglas take
A silver dart, the archer's stake;
Fondly he watch'd, with watery eye,
Some answering glance of sympathy, —
No kind emotion made reply!
Indifferent as to archer wight,
The monarch gave the arrow bright.

XXIII.

Now, clear the ring! for, hand to hand,
The manly wrestlers take their stand.
Two o'er the rest superior rose,
And proud demanded mightier foes,
Nor call'd in vain; for Douglas came. —
For life is Hugh of Larbert lame;
Scarce better John of Alloa's fare,
Whom senseless home his comrades bare.
Prize of the wrestling match, the King
To Douglas gave a golden ring,
While coldly glanced his eye of blue,
As frozen drop of wintry dew.
Douglas would speak, but in his breast
His struggling soul his words suppress'd;
Indignant then he turn'd him where

Their arms the brawny yeomen bare,
To hurl the massive bar in air.
When each his utmost strength had shown,
The Douglas rent an earth-fast stone 650
From its deep bed, then heaved it high,
And sent the fragment through the sky,
A rood beyond the farthest mark; —
And still in Stirling's royal park,
The gray-hair'd sires, who know the past,
To strangers point the Douglas-cast,
And moralize on the decay.
Of Scottish strength in modern day.

XXIV.

The vale with loud applauses rang,
The Ladies' Rock sent back the clang. 660
The King, with look unmoved, bestow'd
A purse well fill'd with pieces broad.
Indignant smiled the Douglas proud,
And threw the gold among the crowd,
Who now, with anxious wonder, scan,
And sharper glance, the dark gray man;
Till whispers rose among the throng,
That heart so free and hand so strong
Must to the Douglas blood belong;
The old men mark'd, and shook the head, 670

To see his hair with silver spread,
And wink'd aside, and told each son
Of feats upon the English done,
Ere Douglas of the stalwart hand
Was exiled from his native land.
The women prais'd his stately form,
Though wreck'd by many a winter's storm;
The youth, with awe and wonder, saw
His strength surpassing Nature's law.
Thus judged, as is their wont, the crowd, 680
Till murmur rose to clamors loud.
But not a glance from that proud ring
Of peers who circled round the King,
With Douglas held communion kind,
Or call'd the banish'd man to mind;
No, not from those who, at the chase,
Once held his side the honor'd place,
Begirt his board, and in the field
Found safety underneath his shield;
For he, whom royal eyes disown, 690
When was his form to courtiers known!

XXV.

The Monarch saw the gambols flag,
And bade let loose a gallant stag,
Whose pride, the holiday to crown,

Two favorite greyhounds should pull down,
That venison free, and Bourdeaux wine,
Might serve the archery to dine.
But Lufra, whom from Douglas' side
Nor bribe nor threat could e'er divide,
The fleetest hound in all the North, — 700
Brave Lufra saw, and darted forth.
She left the royal hounds mid-way,
And, dashing on the antler'd prey,
Sunk her sharp muzzle in his flank,
And deep the flowing life-blood drank.
The King's stout huntsman saw the sport
By strange intruder broken short,
Came up, and, with his leash unbound,
In anger struck the noble hound.
— The Douglas had endured, that morn, 710
The King's cold look, the nobles' scorn,
And last, and worst to spirit proud,
Had borne the pity of the crowd;
But Lufra had been fondly bred,
To share his board, to watch his bed,
And oft would Ellen, Lufra's neck,
In maiden glee, with garlands deck;
They were such playmates that, with name
Of Lufra, Ellen's image came.
His stifled wrath is brimming high, 720
In darken'd brow and flashing eye; —

As waves before the bark divide,
The crowd gave way before his stride;
Needs but a buffet and no more,
The groom lies senseless in his gore.
Such blow no other hand could deal,
Though gauntleted in glove of steel.

XXVI.

Then clamor'd loud the royal train,
And brandish'd swords and staves amain,
But stern the Baron's warning — " Back!
Back, on your lives, ye menial pack!
Beware the Douglas. — Yes! behold,
King James! The Douglas, doom'd of old,
And vainly sought for near and far,
A victim to atone the war,
A willing victim, now attends,
Nor craves thy grace but for his friends." —
" Thus is my clemency repaid?
Presumptuous Lord!" the Monarch said;
" Of thy mis-proud ambitious clan,
Thou, James of Bothwell, wert the man,
The only man, in whom a foe
My woman-mercy would not know;
But shall a Monarch's presence brook
Injurious blow and haughty look? —

What ho! the Captain of our Guard!
Give the offender fitting ward. —
Break off the sports!"— for tumult rose,
And yeomen 'gan to bend their bows, —
" Break off the sports!" he said, and frown'd, 750
" And bid our horsemen clear the ground."—

XXVII.

Then uproar wild and misarray
Marr'd the fair form of festal day.
The horsemen prick'd among the crowd,
Repell'd by threats and insult loud;
To earth are borne the old and weak,
The timorous fly, the women shriek;
With flint, with shaft, with staff, with bar,
The hardier urge tumultuous war.
At once round Douglas darkly sweep 760
The royal spears in circle deep,
And slowly scale the pathway steep;
While on the rear in thunder pour
The rabble with disorder'd roar.
With grief the noble Douglas saw
The Commons rise against the law,
And to the leading soldier said, —
" Sir John of Hyndford! 'twas my blade,
That knighthood on thy shoulder laid;

For that good deed, permit me then 770
A word with these misguided men. —

XXVIII.

"Hear, gentle friends! ere yet for me
Ye break the bands of fealty.
My life, my honor, and my cause,
I tender free to Scotland's laws.
Are these so weak as must require
The aid of your misguided ire?
Or, if I suffer causeless wrong,
Is then my selfish rage so strong,
My sense of public weal so low, 780
That, for mean vengeance on a foe,
Those cords of love I should unbind
Which knit my country and my kind?
O no! Believe, in yonder tower
It will not soothe my captive hour,
To know those spears our foes should dread,
For me in kindred gore are red;
To know, in fruitless brawl begun,
For me that mother wails her son;
For me that widow's mate expires; 790
For me that orphans weep their sires;
That patriots mourn insulted laws,
And curse the Douglas for the cause.

O let your patience ward such ill,
And keep your right to love me still!" —

XXIX.

The crowd's wild fury sunk amain
In tears, as tempests melt in rain.
With lifted hands and eyes, they pray'd
For blessings on his generous head,
Who for his country felt alone,   800
And prized her blood beyond his own.
Old men upon the verge of life
Bless'd him who stay'd the civil strife;
And mothers held their babes on high,
The self-devoted Chief to spy,
Triumphant over wrong and ire,
To whom the prattlers owed a sire:
Even the rough soldier's heart was moved;
As if behind some bier beloved,
With trailing arms and drooping head,   810
The Douglas up the hill he led,
And at the Castle's battled verge,
With sighs resign'd his honor'd charge.

XXX.

The offended Monarch rode apart,
With bitter thought and swelling heart,

And would not now vouchsafe again
Through Stirling streets to lead his train.
"O Lennox, who would wish to rule
This changeling crowd, this common fool?
Hear'st thou," he said, "the loud acclaim 820
With which they shout the Douglas name?
With like acclaim, the vulgar throat
Strain'd for King James their morning note;
With like acclaim they hail'd the day,
When first I broke the Douglas' sway;
And like acclaim would Douglas greet
If he could hurl me from my seat.
Who o'er the herd would wish to reign,
Fantastic, fickle, fierce, and vain!
Vain as the leaf upon the stream, 830
And fickle as a changeful dream;
Fantastic as a woman's mood,
And fierce as Frenzy's fever'd blood.
Thou many-headed monster-thing,
O who would wish to be thy king!—

XXXI.

"But soft! what messenger of speed
Spurs hitherward his panting steed?
I guess his cognizance afar —
What from our cousin, John of Mar?"—
"He prays, my liege, your sports keep bound 840

Within the safe and guarded ground:
For some foul purpose yet unknown, —
Most sure for evil to the throne, —
The outlaw'd Chieftain, Roderick Dhu,
Has summon'd his rebellious crew;
'Tis said, in James of Bothwell's aid
These loose banditti stand array'd.
The Earl of Mar, this morn, from Doune,
To break their muster march'd, and soon
Your grace will hear of battle fought;   850
But earnestly the Earl besought,
Till for such danger he provide,
With scanty train you will not ride."

XXXII.

"Thou warn'st me I have done amiss,
I should have earlier look'd to this:
I lost it in this bustling day. —
Retrace with speed thy former way;
Spare not for spoiling of thy steed,
The best of mine shall be thy meed.
Say to our faithful Lord of Mar,   860
We do forbid the intended war;
Roderick, this morn, in single fight,
Was made our prisoner by a knight;
And Douglas hath himself and cause
Submitted to our kingdom's laws.

The tidings of their leaders lost
Will soon dissolve the mountain host,
Nor would we that the vulgar feel,
For their Chief's crimes, avenging steel.
Bear Mar our message, Braco, fly!" —   870
He turn'd his steed, — "My liege, I hie, —
Yet, ere I cross this lily lawn,
I fear the broadswords will be drawn."
The turf the flying courser spurn'd,
And to his towers the King return'd.

XXXIII.

Ill with King James' mood that day,
Suited gay feast and minstrel lay;
Soon were dismiss'd the courtly throng,
And soon cut short the festal song.
Nor less upon the sadden'd town   880
The evening sunk in sorrow down.
The burghers spoke of civil jar,
Of rumor'd feuds and mountain war,
Of Moray, Mar, and Roderick Dhu,
All up in arms: — the Douglas too,
They mourn'd him pent within the hold,
"Where stout Earl William was of old."
And there his word the speaker staid,
And finger on his lip he laid,
Or pointed to his dagger blade.   890

But jaded horsemen, from the west,
At evening to the castle press'd;
And busy talkers said they bore
Tidings of fight on Katrine's shore;
At noon the deadly fray begun,
And lasted till the set of sun.
Thus giddy rumor shook the town,
Till closed the Night her pennons brown.

CANTO SIXTH.

The Guard-Room.

I.

The sun, awakening, through the smoky air
  Of the dark city casts a sullen glance,
Rousing each caitiff to his task of care,
  Of sinful man the sad inheritance;
Summoning revellers from the lagging dance,
  Scaring the prowling robber to his den;
Gilding on battled tower the warder's lance,
  And warning student pale to leave his pen,
And yield his drowsy eyes to the kind nurse of men.

What various scenes, and, O! what scenes of woe,   10
  Are witness'd by that red and struggling beam!
The fever'd patient, from his pallet low,
  Through crowded hospitals beholds it stream;
  The ruin'd maiden trembles at its gleam,
  The debtor wakes to thought of gyve and jail,
  The love-lorn wretch starts from tormenting dream;
  The wakeful mother, by the glimmering pale,
Trims her sick infant's couch, and soothes his feeble wail.

II.

At dawn the towers of Stirling rang
With soldier-step and weapon-clang,   20
While drums, with rolling note, foretell
Relief to weary sentinel.
Through narrow loop and casement barr'd,
The sunbeams sought the Court of Guard,
And, struggling with the smoky air,
Deaden'd the torches' yellow glare.
In comfortless alliance shone
The lights through arch of blacken'd stone,
And show'd wild shapes in garb of war,
Faces deform'd with beard and scar,   30
All haggard from the midnight watch,
And fever'd with the stern debauch;
For the oak table's massive board,
Flooded with wine, with fragments stored,
And beakers drain'd, and cups o'erthrown,
Show'd in what sport the night had flown.
Some, weary, snored on floor and bench;
Some labor'd still their thirst to quench;
Some, chill'd with watching, spread their hands
O'er the huge chimney's dying brands,   40
While round them, or beside them flung,
At every step their harness rung.

III.

These drew not for their fields the sword,
Like tenants of a feudal lord,
Nor own'd the patriarchal claim
Of Chieftain in their leader's name;
Adventurers they, from far who roved,
To live by battle which they loved.
There the Italian's clouded face,
The swarthy Spaniard's there you trace; 50
The mountain-loving Switzer there
More freely breathed in mountain-air;
The Fleming there despised the soil,
That paid so ill the laborer's toil;
Their rolls show'd French and German name;
And merry England's exiles came,
To share, with ill-conceal'd disdain,
Of Scotland's pay the scanty gain.
All brave in arms, well train'd to wield
The heavy halberd, brand, and shield; 60
In camps licentious, wild, and bold;
In pillage fierce and uncontroll'd;
And now, by holytide and feast,
From rules of discipline released.

IV.

They held debate of bloody fray,
Fought 'twixt Loch Katrine and Achray.

Fierce was their speech, and, 'mid their words,
Their hands oft grappled to their swords;
Nor sunk their tone to spare the ear
Of wounded comrades groaning near,
Whose mangled limbs and bodies gored
Bore token of the mountain sword,
Though, neighboring to the Court of Guard,
Their prayers and feverish wails were heard;
Sad burden to the ruffian joke,
And savage oath by fury spoke! —
At length up-started John of Brent,
A yeoman from the banks of Trent;
A stranger to respect or fear,
In peace a chaser of the deer,
In host a hardy mutineer,
But still the boldest of the crew,
When deed of danger was to do.
He grieved, that day, their games cut short,
And marr'd the dicer's brawling sport,
And shouted loud, "Renew the bowl!
And, while a merry catch I troll,
Let each the buxom chorus bear,
Like brethren of the brand and spear." —

V.

Soldier's Song.

Our vicar still preaches that Peter and Poule 90
Laid a swinging long curse on the bonny brown bowl,
That there's wrath and despair in the jolly black-jack,
And the seven deadly sins in a flagon of sack;
Yet whoop, Barnaby! off with thy liquor,
Drink upsees out, and a fig for the vicar!

Our vicar he calls it damnation to sip
The ripe ruddy dew of a woman's dear lip,
Says that Beelzebub lurks in her kerchief so sly,
And Apollyon shoots darts from her merry black eye;
Yet whoop, Jack! kiss Gillian the quicker, 100
Till she bloom like a rose, and a fig for the vicar!

Our vicar thus preaches — and why should he not?
For the dues of his cure are the placket and pot;
And 'tis right of his office poor laymen to lurch,
Who infringe the domains of our good Mother Church.
Yet whoop, bully-boys! off with your liquor,
Sweet Marjorie's the word, and a fig for the vicar!

VI.

The warder's challenge, heard without,
Staid in mid-roar the merry shout.
A soldier to the portal went, — 110

"Here is old Bertram, sirs, of Ghent;
And, beat for jubilee the drum! —
A maid and minstrel with him come." —
Bertram, a Fleming, gray and scarr'd,
Was entering now the Court of Guard,
A harper with him, and in plaid
All muffled close, a mountain maid,
Who backward shrunk to 'scape the view
Of the loose scene and boisterous crew.
"What news?" they roar'd: — "I only know,
From noon till eve we fought with foe,   121
As wild and as untamable
As the rude mountains where they dwell.
On both sides store of blood is lost,
Nor much success can either boast." —
"But whence thy captives, friend? such spoil
As theirs must needs reward thy toil.
Old dost thou wax, and wars grow sharp;
Thou now hast glee-maiden and harp!
Get thee an ape, and trudge the land,   130
The leader of a juggler band." —

VII.

"No, comrade; — no such fortune mine.
After the fight, these sought our line,
That aged harper and the girl,
And, having audience of the Earl,

Mar bade I should purvey them steed,
And bring them hitherward with speed.
Forbear your mirth and rude alarm,
For none shall do them shame or harm." —
"Hear ye his boast!" cried John of Brent,   140
Ever to strife and jangling bent;
"Shall he strike doe beside our lodge,
And yet the jealous niggard grudge
To pay the forester his fee?
I'll have my share howe'er it be,
Despite of Moray, Mar, or thee." —
Bertram his forward step withstood;
And, burning in his vengeful mood,
Old Allan, though unfit for strife,
Laid hand upon his dagger-knife;   150
But Ellen boldly stepp'd between,
And dropp'd at once the tartan screen.
So, from his morning cloud, appears
The sun of May, through summer tears.
The savage soldiery, amazed,
As on descended angel gazed;
Even hardy Brent, abash'd and tamed,
Stood half admiring, half ashamed.

VIII.

Boldly she spoke, — "Soldiers, attend!
My father was the soldier's friend;   160

Cheer'd him in camps, in marches led,
And with him in the battle bled.
Not from the valiant, or the strong,
Should exile's daughter suffer wrong." —
Answer'd De Brent, most forward still
In every feat or good or ill, —
"I shame me of the part I play'd:
And thou an outlaw's child, poor maid!
An outlaw I by forest laws,
And merry Needwood knows the cause. 170
Poor Rose, — if Rose be living now," —
He wiped his iron eye and brow, —
"Must bear such age, I think, as thou.
Hear ye, my mates; — I go to call
The Captain of our watch to hall:
There lies my halberd on the floor;
And he that steps my halberd o'er,
To do the maid injurious part,
My shaft shall quiver in his heart!
Beware loose speech, or jesting rough: 180
Ye all know John de Brent. Enough." —

IX.

Their Captain came, a gallant young, —
(Of Tullibardine's house he sprung,)
Nor wore he yet the spurs of knight;

THE GUARD-ROOM.

Gay was his mien, his humor light,
And, though by courtesy controll'd,
Forward his speech, his bearing bold.
The high-born maiden ill could brook
The scanning of his curious look
And dauntless eye; — and yet, in sooth,   190
Young Lewis was a generous youth;
But Ellen's lovely face and mien,
Ill suited to the garb and scene,
Might lightly bear construction strange,
And give loose fancy scope to range.
"Welcome to Stirling towers, fair maid!
Come ye to seek a champion's aid,
On palfrey white, with harper hoar,
Like errant damosel of yore?
Does thy high quest a knight require,   200
Or may the venture suit a squire?" —
Her dark eye flash'd; — she paused and sigh'd, —
"O what have I to do with pride! —
— Through scenes of sorrow, shame, and strife,
A suppliant for a father's life,
I crave an audience of the King.
Behold, to back my suit, a ring,
The royal pledge of grateful claims,
Given by the Monarch to Fitz-James."

X.

The signet-ring young Lewis took,   210
With deep respect and alter'd look;
And said, — "This ring our duties own;
And pardon, if to worth unknown,
In semblance mean obscurely veil'd,
Lady, in aught my folly fail'd.
Soon as the day flings wide his gates,
The King shall know what suitor waits.
Please you, meanwhile, in fitting bower
Repose you till his waking hour;
Female attendance shall obey   220
Your hest, for service or array.
Permit I marshal you the way."
But, ere she follow'd, with the grace
And open bounty of her race,
She bade her slender purse be shared
Among the soldiers of the guard.
The rest with thanks their guerdon took;
But Brent, with shy and awkward look,
On the reluctant maiden's hold
Forced bluntly back the proffer'd gold; —   230
"Forgive a haughty English heart,
And O forget its ruder part!
The vacant purse shall be my share,
Which in my barret-cap I'll bear,
Perchance, in jeopardy of war,

Where gayer crests may keep afar." —
With thanks, — 'twas all she could, — the maid
His rugged courtesy repaid.

XI.

When Ellen forth with Lewis went,
Allan made suit to John of Brent: —   240
" My lady safe, O let your grace
Give me to see my master's face!
His minstrel I, — to share his doom
Bound from the cradle to the tomb.
Tenth in descent, since first my sires
Waked for his noble house their lyres,
Nor one of all the race was known
But prized its weal above their own.
With the Chief's birth begins our care;
Our harp must soothe the infant heir,   250
Teach the youth tales of fight, and grace
His earliest feat of field or chase;
In peace, in war, our rank we keep,
We cheer his board, we soothe his sleep,
Nor leave him till we pour our verse,
A doleful tribute! — o'er his hearse.
Then let me share his captive lot;
It is my right — deny it not!" —
" Little we reck," said John of Brent,
" We Southern men, of long descent;   260

Nor wot we how a name — a word —
Makes clansmen vassals to a lord:
Yet kind my noble landlord's part, —
God bless the house of Beaudesert!
And, but I loved to drive the deer,
More than to guide the laboring steer,
I had not dwelt an outcast here.
Come, good old Minstrel, follow me;
Thy Lord and Chieftain shalt thou see." —

XII.

Then, from a rusted iron hook, 270
A bunch of ponderous keys he took,
Lighted a torch, and Allan led
Through grated arch and passage dread.
Portals they pass'd, where, deep within,
Spoke prisoner's moan and fetters' din;
Through rugged vaults, where, loosely stored,
Lay wheel, and axe, and headsman's sword,
And many an hideous engine grim,
For wrenching joint, and crushing limb,
By artist form'd, who deem'd it shame 280
And sin to give their work a name.
They halted at a low-brow'd porch,
And Brent to Allan gave the torch,
While bolt and chain he backward roll'd,
And made the bar unhasp its hold.

They enter'd : — 'twas a prison-room
Of stern security and gloom,
Yet not a dungeon; for the day
Through lofty gratings found its way,
And rude and antique garniture   290
Deck'd the sad walls and oaken floor;
Such as the rugged days of old
Deem'd fit for captive noble's hold.
"Here," said De Brent, " thou may'st remain
Till the Leech visit him again.
Strict is his charge, the warders tell,
To tend the noble prisoner well."
Retiring then the bolt he drew,
And the lock's murmurs growl'd anew.
Roused at the sound, from lowly bed   300
A captive feebly raised his head ;
The wondering Minstrel look'd, and knew —
Not his dear Lord, but Roderick Dhu!
For, come from where Clan-Alpine fought,
They, erring, deem'd the Chief he sought.

XIII.

As the tall ship, whose lofty prore
Shall never stem the billows more,
Deserted by her gallant band,
Amid the breakers lies astrand, —
So, on his couch, lay Roderick Dhu!   310

And oft his fever'd limbs he threw
In toss abrupt, as when her sides
Lie rocking in the advancing tides,
That shake her frame with ceaseless beat,
Yet cannot heave her from her seat; —
O! how unlike her course at sea!
Or his free step on hill and lea! —
Soon as the Minstrel he could scan,
— " What of thy lady ? — of my clan ? —
My mother ? — Douglas ? — tell me all! 320
Have they been ruin'd in my fall ?
Ah, yes! or wherefore art thou here ?
Yet speak, — speak boldly, — do not fear." —
(For Allan, who his mood well knew,
Was choked with grief and terror too.)
" Who fought—who fled ? — Old man, be brief ; —
Some might — for they had lost their Chief.
Who basely live ? — who bravely died ? "
" O, calm thee, Chief ! " the Minstrel cried,
" Ellen is safe ; " — " For that, thank Heaven ! " —
" And hopes are for the Douglas given ; — 331
The Lady Margaret too is well ;
And, for thy clan, — on field or fell,
Has never harp of minstrel told
Of combat fought so true and bold.
Thy stately Pine is yet unbent,
Though many a goodly bough is rent."

XIV.

The Chieftain rear'd his form on high,
And fever's fire was in his eye;
But ghastly, pale, and livid streaks 340
Chequer'd his swarthy brow and cheeks.
— "Hark, Minstrel! I have heard thee play,
With measure bold, on festal day,
In yon lone isle, ... again where ne'er
Shall harper play, or warrior hear! . . . .
That stirring air that peals on high,
O'er Dermid's race our victory. —
Strike it! — and then, (for well thou canst,)
Free from thy minstrel-spirit glanced,
Fling me the picture of the fight, 350
When met my clan the Saxon might.
I'll listen, till my fancy hears
The clang of swords, the crash of spears!
These grates, these walls, shall vanish then,
For the fair field of fighting men,
And my free spirit burst away,
As if it soar'd from battle fray."
The trembling Bard with awe obey'd, —
Slow on the harp his hand he laid;
But soon remembrance of the sight 360
He witness'd from the mountain's height,
With what old Bertram told at night,
Awaken'd the full power of song,

And bore him in career along; —
As shallop launch'd on river's tide,
That slow and fearful leaves the side,
But, when it feels the middle stream,
Drives downward swift as lightning's beam.

XV.

Battle of Beal' an Duine.

"The Minstrel came once more to view
The eastern ridge of Benvenue, 370
For ere he parted, he would say
Farewell to lovely Loch Achray —
Where shall he find, in foreign land,
So lone a lake, so sweet a strand! —
  There is no breeze upon the fern,
    Nor ripple on the lake,
  Upon her eyrie nods the erne,
    The deer has sought the brake;
  The small birds will not sing aloud,
    The springing trout lies still, 380
  So darkly glooms yon thunder cloud,
  That swathes, as with a purple shroud,
    Benledi's distant hill.
Is it the thunder's solemn sound
    That mutters deep and dread,
Or echoes from the groaning ground
    The warrior's measured tread?

Is it the lightning's quivering glance
    That on the thicket streams,
Or do they flash on spear and lance
    The sun's retiring beams? —
I see the dagger-crest of Mar,
I see the Moray's silver star,
Wave o'er the cloud of Saxon war,
That up the lake comes winding far!
    To hero bound for battle-strife,
        Or bard of martial lay,
    'Twere worth ten years of peaceful life,
        One glance at their array!

XVI.

" Their light-arm'd archers far and near
    Survey'd the tangled ground,
Their centre ranks, with pike and spear,
    A twilight forest frown'd,
Their barbed horsemen, in the rear,
    The stern battalia crown'd.
No cymbal clash'd, no clarion rang,
    Still were the pipe and drum;
Save heavy tread, and armor's clang,
    The sullen march was dumb.
There breathed no wind their crests to shake,
    Or wave their flags abroad;

Scarce the frail aspen seem'd to quake,
    That shadow'd o'er their road.
Their vaward scouts no tidings bring,
    Can rouse no lurking foe,
Nor spy a trace of living thing,
    Save when they stirr'd the roe;
The host moves, like a deep-sea wave,
Where rise no rocks its pride to brave,
    High-swelling, dark, and slow.   420
The lake is pass'd, and now they gain
A narrow and a broken plain,
Before the Trosachs' rugged jaws:
And here the horse and spearmen pause,
While, to explore the dangerous glen,
Dive through the pass the archer-men.

XVII.

"At once there rose so wild a yell
Within that dark and narrow dell,
As all the fiends from heaven that fell
Had peal'd the banner-cry of hell!   430
    Forth from the pass in tumult driven,
    Like chaff before the wind of heaven,
        The archery appear:
    For life! for life! their plight they ply —
    And shriek, and shout, and battle-cry,

And plaids and bonnets waving high,
And broadswords flashing to the sky,
   Are maddening in the rear.
Onward they drive, in dreadful race,
   Pursuers and pursued;   440
Before that tide of flight and chase,
How shall it keep its rooted place,
   The spearmen's twilight wood? —
' Down, down,' cried Mar, ' your lances down!
   Bear back both friend and foe!' —
Like reeds before the tempest's frown,
That serried grove of lances brown
   At once lay levell'd low;
And closely shouldering side to side,
The bristling ranks the onset bide. —   450
' We'll quell the savage mountaineer,
   As their Tinchel cows the game!
They come as fleet as forest deer,
   We'll drive them back as tame.' —

XVIII.

" Bearing before them, in their course,
The relics of the archer force,
Like wave with crest of sparkling foam,
Right onward did Clan-Alpine come.
   Above the tide, each broadsword bright

Was brandishing like beam of light, 460
　　Each targe was dark below;
And with the ocean's mighty swing,
When heaving to the tempest's wing,
　　They hurl'd them on the foe.
I heard the lance's shivering crash,
As when the whirlwind rends the ash;
I heard the broadsword's deadly clang,
As if an hundred anvils rang!
But Moray wheel'd his rearward rank
Of horsemen on Clan-Alpine's flank,— 470
　　'My banner-man, advance!
I see,' he cried, 'their column shake.
Now, gallants! for your ladies' sake,
　　Upon them with the lance!'—
The horsemen dash'd among the rout,
　　As deer break through the broom;
Their steeds are stout, their swords are out,
　　They soon make lightsome room.
Clan-Alpine's best are backward borne—
　　Where, where was Roderick then! 480
One blast upon his bugle-horn
　　Were worth a thousand men.
And refluent through the pass of fear
　　The battle's tide was pour'd;
Vanish'd the Saxon's struggling spear,
　　Vanish'd the mountain-sword.

As Bracklinn's chasm, so black and steep,
   Receives her roaring linn,
As the dark caverns of the deep
   Suck the wild whirlpool in,
So did the deep and darksome pass
Devour the battle's mingled mass:
None linger now upon the plain,
Save those who ne'er shall fight again.

XIX.

"Now westward rolls the battle's din,
That deep and doubling pass within. —
Minstrel, away! the work of fate
Is bearing on: its issue wait,
Where the rude Trosachs' dread defile
Opens on Katrine's lake and isle. —
Gray Benvenue I soon repass'd,
Loch Katrine lay beneath me cast.
   The sun is set; — the clouds are met,
     The lowering scowl of heaven
   An inky hue of livid blue
     To the deep lake has given;
Strange gusts of wind from mountain glen
Swept o'er the lake, then sunk agen.
I heeded not the eddying surge,
Mine eye but saw the Trosachs' gorge,

Mine ear but heard the sullen sound,
Which like an earthquake shook the ground,
And spoke the stern and desperate strife
That parts not but with parting life,
Seeming, to minstrel ear, to toll
The dirge of many a passing soul.
    Nearer it comes — the dim-wood glen
    The martial flood disgorged agen,
      But not in mingled tide;
    The plaided warriors of the North   520
    High on the mountain thunder forth
      And overhang its side;
    While by the lake below appears
    The dark'ning cloud of Saxon spears.
    At weary bay each shatter'd band,
    Eyeing their foemen, sternly stand;
    Their banners stream like tatter'd sail,
    That flings its fragments to the gale,
    And broken arms and disarray
    Mark'd the fell havoc of the day.   530

XX.

"Viewing the mountain's ridge askance,
The Saxon stood in sullen trance,
Till Moray pointed with his lance,
    And cried — 'Behold yon isle! —
See! none are left to guard its strand,

THE GUARD-ROOM.

But women weak, that wring the hand:
'Tis there of yore the robber band
    Their booty wont to pile; —
My purse, with bonnet-pieces store,
To him will swim a bow-shot o'er,   540
And loose a shallop from the shore.
Lightly we'll tame the war-wolf then,
Lords of his mate, and brood, and den.' —
Forth from the ranks a spearman sprung,
On earth his casque and corslet rung,
    He plunged him in the wave: —
All saw the deed — the purpose knew,
And to their clamors Benvenue
    A mingled echo gave;
The Saxons shout, their mate to cheer,   550
The helpless females scream for fear,
And yells for rage the mountaineer.
'Twas then, as by the outcry riven,
Pour'd down at once the lowering heaven;
A whirlwind swept Loch Katrine's breast,
Her billows rear'd their snowy crest.
Well for the swimmer swell'd they high,
To mar the Highland marksman's eye;
For round him shower'd, 'mid rain and hail,
The vengeful arrows of the Gael. —   560
In vain — He nears the isle — and lo!
His hand is on a shallop's bow.

Just then a flash of lightning came,
It tinged the waves and strand with flame; —
I mark'd Duncraggan's widow'd dame,
Behind an oak I saw her stand,
A naked dirk gleam'd in her hand: —
It darken'd, — but amid the moan
Of waves, I heard a dying groan; —
Another flash! — the spearman floats
A weltering corse beside the boats,
And the stern matron o'er him stood,
Her hand and dagger streaming blood.

XXI.

"'Revenge! revenge!' the Saxons cried,
The Gaels' exulting shout replied.
Despite the elemental rage,
Again they hurried to engage;
But, ere they closed in desperate fight,
Bloody with spurring came a knight,
Sprung from his horse, and, from a crag,
Waved 'twixt the hosts a milk-white flag.
Clarion and trumpet by his side
Rung forth a truce-note high and wide,
While, in the Monarch's name, afar
An herald's voice forbade the war,
For Bothwell's lord, and Roderick bold,

Were both, he said, in captive hold." —
But here the lay made sudden stand,
The harp escaped the Minstrel's hand!
Oft had he stolen a glance, to spy 590
How Roderick brook'd his minstrelsy:
At first, the Chieftain, to the chime,
With lifted hand kept feeble time;
That motion ceased, — yet feeling strong
Varied his look as changed the song;
At length, no more his deafen'd ear
The minstrel melody can hear;
His face grows sharp, — his hands are clench'd,
As if some pang his heart-strings wrench'd;
Set are his teeth, his fading eye 600
Is sternly fix'd on vacancy;
Thus, motionless and moanless, drew
His parting breath, stout Roderick Dhu! —
Old Allan-bane look'd on aghast,
While grim and still his spirit pass'd;
But when he saw that life was fled,
He pour'd his wailing o'er the dead.

XXII.

Lament.

" And art thou cold, and lowly laid,
Thy foemen's dread, thy people's aid,

Breadalbane's boast, Clan-Alpine's shade! 610
For thee shall none a requiem say? —
For thee, — who loved the minstrel's lay,
For thee, of Bothwell's house the stay,
The shelter of her exiled line,
E'en in this prison-house of thine,
I'll wail for Alpine's honor'd Pine!

"What groans shall yonder valleys fill!
What shrieks of grief shall rend yon hill!
What tears of burning rage shall thrill,
When mourns thy tribe thy battles done, 620
Thy fall before the race was won,
Thy sword ungirt ere set of sun!
There breathes not clansman of thy line,
But would have given his life for thine. —
O woe for Alpine's honor'd Pine!

"Sad was thy lot on mortal stage! —
The captive thrush may brook the cage,
The prison'd eagle dies for rage.
Brave spirit, do not scorn my strain!
And, when its notes awake again, 630
Even she, so long beloved in vain,
Shall with my harp her voice combine,
And mix her woe and tears with mine,
To wail Clan-Alpine's honor'd Pine." —

XXIII.

Ellen, the while, with bursting heart,
Remain'd in lordly bower apart,
Where play'd, with many-color'd gleams,
Through storied pane the rising beams.
In vain on gilded roof they fall,
And lighten'd up a tapestried wall,
And for her use a menial train
A rich collation spread in vain.
The banquet proud, the chamber gay,
Scarce drew one curious glance astray;
Or if she look'd, 'twas but to say,
With better omen dawn'd the day
In that lone isle, where waved on high
The dun-deer's hide for canopy;
Where oft her noble father shared
The simple meal her care prepared,
While Lufra, crouching by her side,
Her station claim'd with jealous pride,
And Douglas, bent on woodland game,
Spoke of the chase to Malcolm Græme,
Whose answer, oft at random made,
The wandering of his thoughts betray'd. —
Those who such simple joys have known,
Are taught to prize them when they're gone.
But sudden, see, she lifts her head,
The window seeks with cautious tread.

What distant music has the power
To win her in this woful hour!
'Twas from a turret that o'erhung
Her latticed bower, the strain was sung.

XXIV.

Lay of the Imprisoned Huntsman.

"My hawk is tired of perch and hood,
My idle greyhound loathes his food,
My horse is weary of his stall,
And I am sick of captive thrall.
I wish I were as I have been,
Hunting the hart in forests green,   670
With bended bow and bloodhound free,
For that's the life is meet for me.
I hate to learn the ebb of time
From yon dull steeple's drowsy chime,
Or mark it as the sunbeams crawl,
Inch after inch, along the wall.
The lark was wont my matins ring,
The sable rook my vespers sing;
These towers, although a king's they be,
Have not a hall of joy for me.   680
No more at dawning morn I rise,
And sun myself in Ellen's eyes,
Drive the fleet deer the forest through,
And homeward wend with evening dew;

A blithesome welcome blithely meet,
And lay my trophies at her feet,
While fled the eve on wing of glee, —
That life is lost to love and me!" —

XXV.

The heart-sick lay was hardly said,
The list'ner had not turn'd her head, 690
It trickled still, the starting tear,
When light a footstep struck her ear,
And Snowdoun's graceful Knight was near.
She turn'd the hastier, lest again
The prisoner should renew his strain.
"O welcome, brave Fitz-James!" she said;
"How may an almost orphan maid
Pay the deep debt" — "O say not so!
To me no gratitude you owe.
Not mine, alas! the boon to give, 700
And bid thy noble father live;
I can but be thy guide, sweet maid,
With Scotland's King thy suit to aid.
No tyrant he, though ire and pride
May lay his better mood aside.
Come, Ellen, come! 'tis more than time,
He holds his court at morning prime."
With beating heart, and bosom wrung,
As to a brother's arm she clung.

Gently he dried the falling tear,   710
And gently whisper'd hope and cheer;
Her faltering steps half led, half staid,
Through gallery fair and high arcade,
Till, at his touch, its wings of pride
A portal arch unfolded wide.

XXVI.

Within 'twas brilliant all and light,
A thronging scene of figures bright;
It glow'd on Ellen's dazzled sight,
As when the setting sun has given
Ten thousand hues to summer even,   720
And, from their tissue, fancy frames
Aerial knights and fairy dames.
Still by Fitz-James her footing staid;
A few faint steps she forward made,
Then slow her drooping head she raised,
And fearful round the presence gazed;
For him she sought who own'd this state,
The dreaded Prince whose will was fate! —
She gazed on many a princely port,
Might well have ruled a royal court;   730
On many a splendid garb she gazed, —
Then turn'd bewilder'd and amazed,
For all stood bare; and, in the room,
Fitz-James alone wore cap and plume.

To him each lady's look was lent,
On him each courtier's eye was bent;
Midst furs and silks and jewels sheen,
He stood, in simple Lincoln green,
The centre of the glittering ring, —
And Snowdoun's Knight is Scotland's King! 740

XXVII.

As wreath of snow on mountain-breast
Slides from the rock that gave it rest,
Poor Ellen glided from her stay,
And at the Monarch's feet she lay;
No word her choking voice commands, —
She show'd the ring, — she clasp'd her hands.
O not a moment could he brook,
The generous Prince, that suppliant look!
Gently he raised her, — and, the while,
Check'd with a glance the circle's smile; 750
Graceful, but grave, her brow he kiss'd,
And bade her terrors be dismiss'd: —
"Yes, Fair; the wandering poor Fitz-James
The fealty of Scotland claims.
To him thy woes, thy wishes, bring;
He will redeem his signet ring.
Ask naught for Douglas; — yester even,
His Prince and he have much forgiven:
Wrong hath he had from slanderous tongue,

I, from his rebel kinsmen, wrong. 760
We would not, to the vulgar crowd,
Yield what they craved with clamor loud;
Calmly we heard and judged his cause,
Our council aided, and our laws.
I stanch'd thy father's death-feud stern,
With stout De Vaux and gray Glencairn;
And Bothwell's Lord henceforth we own
The friend and bulwark of our Throne. —
But, lovely infidel, how now?
What clouds thy misbelieving brow? — 770
Lord James of Douglas, lend thine aid;
Thou must confirm this doubting maid." —

XXVIII.

Then forth the noble Douglas sprung,
And on his neck his daughter hung.
The monarch drank, that happy hour,
The sweetest, holiest draught of Power, —
When it can say, with godlike voice,
Arise, sad Virtue, and rejoice!
Yet would not James the general eye
On Nature's raptures long should pry; 780
He stepp'd between — "Nay, Douglas, nay,
Steal not my proselyte away!
The riddle 'tis my right to read,
That brought this happy chance to speed. —

Yes, Ellen, when disguised I stray
In life's more low but happier way,
'Tis under name which veils my power,
Nor falsely veils — for Stirling's tower
Of yore the name of Snowdoun claims,
And Normans call me James Fitz-James.   790
Thus watch I o'er insulted laws,
Thus learn to right the injured cause."
Then, in a tone apart and low, —
"Ah, little traitress! none must know
What idle dream, what lighter thought,
What vanity full dearly bought,
Join'd to thine eye's dark witchcraft, drew
My spell-bound steps to Benvenue
In dangerous hour, and all but gave
Thy monarch's life to mountain glaive!" —   800
Aloud he spoke — "Thou still dost hold
That little talisman of gold,
Pledge of my faith, Fitz-James's ring —
What seeks fair Ellen of the King?"

XXIX.

Full well the conscious maiden guess'd
He prob'd the weakness of her breast;
But, with that consciousness, there came
A lightening of her fears for Græme,
And more she deem'd the monarch's ire

Kindled 'gainst him, who, for her sire,
Rebellious broadsword boldly drew;
And, to her generous feeling true,
She craved the grace of Roderick Dhu.
"Forbear thy suit: — the King of kings
Alone can stay life's parting wings.
I know his heart, I know his hand,
Have shared his cheer, and proved his brand; —
My fairest earldom would I give
To bid Clan-Alpine's Chieftain live! —
Hast thou no other boon to crave?
No other captive friend to save?"
Blushing, she turn'd her from the King,
And to the Douglas gave the ring,
As if she wish'd her sire to speak
The suit that stain'd her glowing cheek. —
"Nay, then, my pledge has lost its force,
And stubborn justice holds her course.
Malcolm, come forth!" — and, at the word,
Down kneel'd the Græme to Scotland's Lord.
"For thee, rash youth, no suppliant sues,
From thee may Vengeance claim her dues,
Who, nurtured underneath our smile,
Hast paid our care by treacherous wile,
And sought, amid thy faithful clan,
A refuge for an outlaw'd man,
Dishonoring thus thy loyal name. —

Fetters and warder for the Græme!"—
His chain of gold the King unstrung,
The links o'er Malcolm's neck he flung,
Then gently drew the glittering band, 840
And laid the clasp on Ellen's hand.

———

HARP of the North, farewell! The hills grow dark,
   On purple peaks a deeper shade descending;
In twilight copse the glow-worm lights her spark,
   The deer, half-seen, are to the covert wending.
Resume thy wizard elm! the fountain lending,
   And the wild breeze, thy wilder minstrelsy;
Thy numbers sweet with Nature's vespers blending,
   With distant echo from the fold and lea,
And herd-boy's evening pipe, and hum of housing bee.

Yet, once again, farewell, thou Minstrel Harp! 851
   Yet, once again, forgive my feeble sway,
And little reck I of the censure sharp
   May idly cavil at an idle lay.
Much have I owed thy strains on life's long way,
   Through secret woes the world has never known,
When on the weary night dawn'd wearier day,
   And bitterer was the grief devour'd alone.
That I o'erlive such woes, Enchantress! is thine own.

Hark! as my lingering footsteps slow retire,   860
   Some Spirit of the Air has waked thy string!
'Tis now a Seraph bold, with touch of fire,
   'Tis now the brush of Fairy's frolic wing.
Receding now, the dying numbers ring
   Fainter and fainter down the rugged dell,
And now the mountain breezes scarcely bring
   A wandering witch-note of the distant spell —
And now, 'tis silent all! — Enchantress, fare thee well!

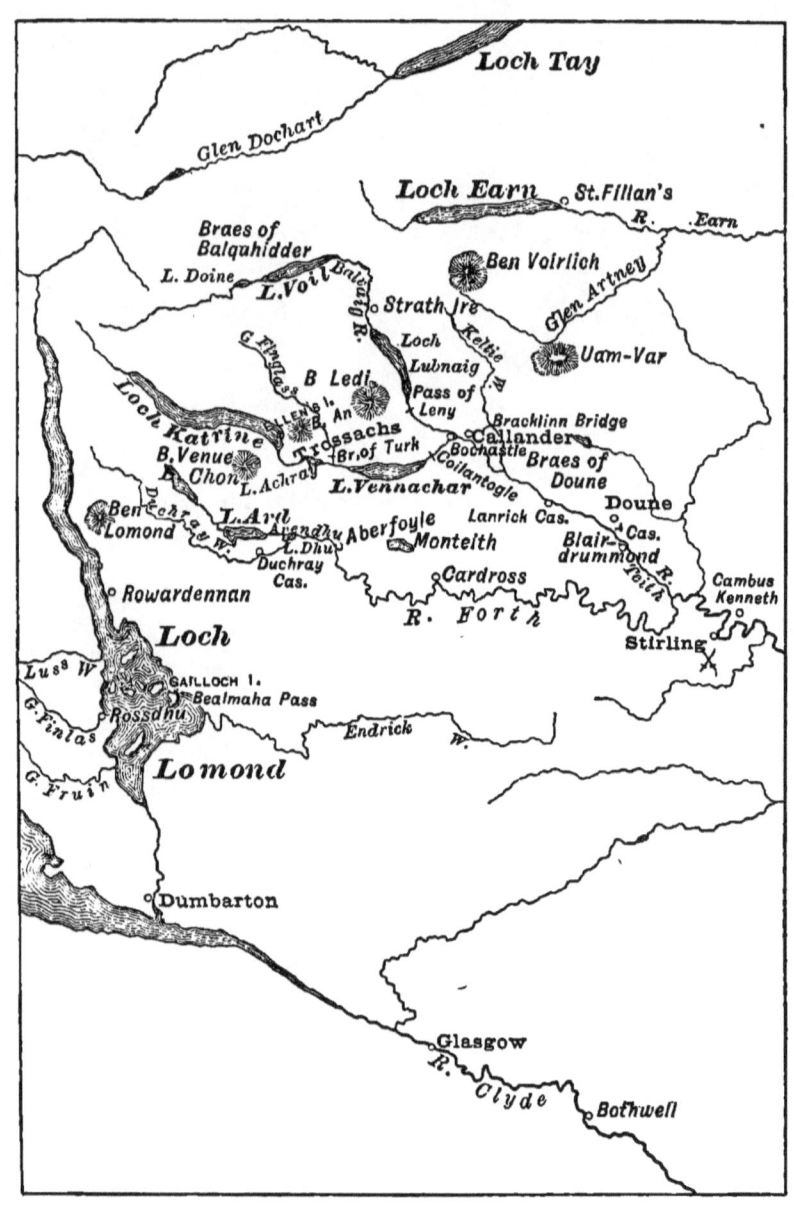

NOTES ON THE LADY OF THE LAKE.

CANTO FIRST.
The Chase.
ABBREVIATIONS.

Cf. = *confer*, compare.
i.e. = *id est*, that is.
e.g. = *exempli gratia*, for example.

Each canto begins with one or more Spenserian stanzas, so called because first used by Edmund Spenser. The Spenserian stanza consists of nine lines, the prevailing foot being the iambus (two syllables, with the accent on the second). The first eight lines have five feet (iambic pentameter); the ninth line has six feet (iambic hexameter), and is called an Alexandrine. The first and third lines rhyme, the second, fourth, fifth, and seventh, and the sixth, eighth, and ninth. The metre of the poem proper is iambic tetrameter; that is, the prevailing foot is the iambus, and there are four feet in the line. (See Parsons's " English Versification.")

2. **Witch-elm ;** i.e., the drooping or bending elm.
Saint Fillan was a famous Scotch saint of the seventh century.
"Thence to Saint Fillan's blessed well,
  Whose springs can frenzied dreams dispel,
    And the crazed brain restore." — *Marmion*, i. 29.

4. **Envious ivy.** Envious of the musical powers of the harp.
10. **Caledon.** Caledonia was the ancient name of Scotland.
14. **According pause.** Each pause in the song was filled by the according music of the harp.
17. **Burden ;** i.e., the subject.
20. **Thy magic maze.** Maze, labyrinth. Applied to the harp on account of the confusing variety of sounds.
29. **Monan's rill.** Saint Monan was a Scotch martyr of the fourth century.

31. **Glenartney's.** A *glen* along the Artney River, between Benvoirlich on the north and Uam-Var on the south. (See map.)
33. **Benvoirlich's.** *Ben* in Gaelic means mountain.
35. Observe the alliteration in this and other lines. (See Parsons's " English Versification.")
38. Observe that the simile comes before the object it illustrates. (See vi. 741 and note.)
42. **Ere.** Good in poetry, not in prose. Other examples found in this poem are *adown, perforce, fain, yon, erst, happed, steepy,* etc.
45. **Beamed frontlet.** Forehead well furnished with horns.
47. **Tainted** with the scent of his pursuers.
48. **Cry.** Properly the yelping of the hounds, but sometimes the pack of hounds.
49. **Chase.** Sometimes the act of pursuit, sometimes the thing pursued, but here the pursuers.
53. **Uam-Var.** The name signifies the great den or cavern.
54. Upon obtaining a view of the stag, the pack of hounds burst into cry.
55. **Paid them back.** Echoed. Notice the spirited description of the echo.
58. **An.** Not now used before *h* pronounced, unless the word is accented on the second syllable.
66. **Cairn.** A heap of stones.
67. **Rout.** (1) Defeat. (2) A troop or crowd of people. (See Skeat's " Etymological Dictionary.")
69. **Hurricane;** i.e., the wild rush of hunters, horses, and hounds.
71. **Linn.** A pool or cascade. Cf. **Bracklinn,** ii. 270.
84. **Shrewdly.** Severely. (See Skeat's " Etymological Dictionary.")
89. **Menteith.** The country of the River Teith.
90. **Lochard;** i.e., Loch Ard. **Aberfoyle.** Cf. *Aberdeen. Aber* means a confluence.
102. **'Twere.** It would be.
103. **Cambusmore.** Two miles from Callander.
105. **Benledi.** " Mountain of God," nearly 3,000 feet high.
111. **Vennachar.** " Lake of the Fair Valley."
112. **Brigg of Turk.** This bridge was " the scene of the death of a wild boar famous in Celtic tradition."

115. **Scourge and steel.** Whip and spur. In *steel* for *spur* (elsewhere for *sword*) we have material put for the thing, — metonymy.

120. **Saint Hubert's breed.** The abbots of Saint Hubert kept some of this black breed in honor of the saint, who was a hunter.

122. **Flying traces.** Notice the transferrence of the epithet *flying* from the stag to the track that he leaves behind him.

127. **Quarry.** The hunted animal.

130. **Stock.** Stump.

133. **Turn to bay.** Turn and face the hounds.

137. **Death-wound.** "When the stag turned to bay, the ancient hunter had the perilous task of going in upon, and killing or disabling, the desperate animal. At certain times of the year this was held particularly dangerous, a wound received from a stag's horn being then deemed poisonous, and more dangerous than one from the tusks of a boar. . . . At all times, however, the task was dangerous, and to be adventured upon wisely and warily, either by getting behind the stag while he was gazing on the hounds, or by watching an opportunity to gallop roundly in upon him, and kill him with the sword." —*Scott.*

138. **Whinyard.** A short sword. Cf. *whinger* and *hanger*.

142. **Turn'd him** would be turned *himself* in prose.

145. **Trosachs, or Trossachs,** means "the rough or bristled territory," especially the pass between Loch Katrine and Loch Vennachar.

150. **Amain.** With main force. Cf. *might and main*.

151. **Chiding.** Cf. **chide,** l. 287.

163. **Banks of Seine.** James visited France in 1536.

166. **Woe worth.** Woe be to.

184, etc. Notice the accurate and minute description. "Landscape Painting in Poetry."

"He sees everything with a painter's eye. Whatever he represents has a character of individuality, and is drawn with an accuracy and minuteness of discrimination which we are not accustomed to expect from mere verbal description. It is because Mr. Scott usually delineates those objects with which he is perfectly familiar that his touch is so easy, correct, and animated. The rocks, the ravines, and the torrents which he exhibits are not the imperfect sketches of a hurried traveller, but the finished studies of a resident artist." — *Quarterly Review,* May, 1810.

See l. 278, note.

193. **Thunder-splinter'd;** i.e., lightning-splintered. Cf. *thunder-bolt, thunder-struck.*

196, 197. **The tower ... on Shinar's plain.** The tower of Babel. (See Genesis xi. 1-9.)

202. **Pagod** = pagoda. Crests *as* wild as.

208. **Sheen** is here an adjective; bright. It is sometimes a noun; brightness.

212. **Boon.** Bountiful.

217. **Clift** is the reading of the first editions; later editions have **cliff. Bower.** A retired chamber or room.

218, 219. See Ruskin's "Modern Painters," vol. iii.

222, 223. An imperfect rhyme, not to be explained by peculiarity of Scotch pronunciation. Cf. 224, 225, 256, 257, 435, 436, 445, 456. See Parsons's "English Versification," ch. vi.

227. **Frequent.** This use of adjective for adverb is common in poetry. See 266 and elsewhere.

231. **Streamers** of the rose, the ivy, or other vines.

238. **Brim.** Properly the edge, border, but here the surface.

239. **To swim** = for swimming. Cf. **to rise,** l. 159.

240, 241. **Lost, veering, broader,** all refer to inlet, l. 237. This loose construction would not do in prose.

245. **Its.** The inlet's.

256. **Nice.** Observe the correct meaning here. For rhyme see note on ll. 222, 223.

267. **Livelier.** "Because in motion?" or "brighter as distinguished from the darker purple of the islands?"

272. **Confusedly.** Three syllables.

274. **Wildering.** Bewildering. See 434.

278, etc. "Perhaps the art of landscape-painting in poetry has never been displayed in higher perfection than in these stanzas, to which rigid criticism might possibly object that the picture is somewhat too minute, and that the contemplation of it detains the traveller somewhat too long from the main purpose of his pilgrimage, but which it would be an act of the greatest injustice to break into fragments and present by piecemeal. Not so the magnificent scene which bursts upon the bewildered hunter as he emerges at length from the dell, and commands at one view the beautiful expanse of Loch Katrine." — *Critical Review,* August, 1820.

287. **Chide.** See l. 151.

302. **Beshrew.** Curse (mildly).
317. **Fall** = befall, happen.
319. **Wound.** *Winded* would be the better form. The same is true of iii. 15. See 1. 500.
322. **Islet** and *isle* in poetry; *island* in prose.
342. **Naiad.** Water-nymph.
363. **Snood.** See iii. 114. **Plaid.** A perfect rhyme.
377. **Confess'd.** Bore witness to. Not the modern meaning.
389. **Silent horn.** Silence of the horn; impatient because the horn is silent. Cf. ii. 776, **punishment delay'd.**
401. **Between.** Here an adverb.
408. **Wont.** Are wont, or accustomed. Now obsolete as a verb.
409. **Middle age.** James was only thirty when he died.
413. **Frolic.** The adjective is now *frolicsome*.
420. **Blade.** Sword. A part for the whole, — synecdoche.
434. **Wilder'd.** Bewildered; lost in the *wilds*, or wilderness. See 274.
441. **Mere.** Lake. Cf. *Windermere*.
443. **Rood.** Cross; crucifix.
449. For another instance of **fair** used as a noun, see ii. 80.
457. **Yesternight.** Obsolete; but we still have *fortnight* and *yesterday*.
464. **Lincoln green.** Green cloth made in Lincoln.
475. **Errant-Knight.** Knight-errant is the correct form now.
476. **Sooth.** Here an adjective meaning true. Cf. *forsooth, in sooth*.
478. **Front** = confront, face. **Emprise.** Enterprise.
481. **Frigate.** Properly a large vessel.
489. **Behind.** Here an adverb. Cf. **between, 401.**
492. **Rocky isle.** "It is a little island, but very famous in Romance-land as 'Ellen's Isle;' for Ellen, as almost everybody knows, was the name of the Lady of the Lake. . . . It is mostly composed of dark gray rocks, mottled with pale and gray lichens, peeping out here and there amid trees that mantle them, — chiefly light, graceful birches, intermingled with red-berried mountain ashes, and a few dark-green, spiry pines. . . . A more poetic, romantic retreat could hardly be imagined; it is unique. It is completely hidden, not only by the trees, but also by an undergrowth of beautiful and abundant ferns, and the loveliest of heather." — Hunnewell's *Lands of Scott*.

496. That neither track nor pathway might declare.
500. **Winded.** We should expect *wound*. See l. 319, and v. 22.
506, 507. Not a perfect rhyme.
525. **Idæan vine.** Some say that this is the *vitis Idæa*, or red whortleberry; others say that it is the common vine, and that *Idæan* is simply the adjective formed from Ida, a mountain near ancient Troy, famous for its vines.
528. Observe the elipsis of *that*, or *which*, before **could bear.**
536, 537. For the omen, see ii. 309, 310.
546. **Target.** Cf. **targe**, iii. 445, v. 380.
548. **Arrows store** = store (i.e., plenty) of arrows. Cf. iii. 3, and vi. 124.
558. **Tapestry.** Here two syllables.
566. **Brook.** Endure.
573. **Ferragus or Ascabart.** Two giants in old romance, one forty, and the other thirty, feet tall.
574. **Hold** = stronghold.
581. For the exact relationship, see ii. 252.
585. " The Highlanders, who carried hospitality to a punctilious excess, are said to have considered it as churlish to ask a stranger his name or lineage before he had taken refreshment. Feuds were so frequent among them, that a contrary rule would in many cases have produced the discovery of some circumstance which might have excluded the guest from the benefit of the assistance he stood in need of." — *Scott*.
591. **Snowdoun.** Stirling Castle. **James Fitz-James.** James the son of James.
592. **Barren.** On account of the misfortunes of the earlier Jameses, and the internal feuds of Scotch chiefs.
596. **Wot** = knows. From obsolete verb, of which the infinitive *to wit*, is still found in legal forms.
598. If any particular **Lord Moray** is meant, probably it is James Stewart, a natural son of James IV., and brother of James V.
602. **Require** = request.
616. Observe the alliteration. **Weird.** Skilled in witchcraft. **Down** = hill.
624. Observe the change to trochaic metre; that is, the prevailing foot is a trochee, — an accented, followed by an unaccented, syllable.
629. For the material of the couch, see ll. 437, 438, and 667.

NOTES ON THE LADY OF THE LAKE. 225

631. **Dewing** = bedewing. Cf. **wilder'd,** 1. 434.
638. **Pibroch.** Strictly a Highland air, usually played on the bagpipe; but here it means the bagpipe.
642. **Bittern.** A marsh bird; small heron.
646. **Here's.** Would be *here are* in prose.
648. **Led the lay.** Gave the song a new turn.
657. Notice the ellipsis of *that*. **Reveillé.** Awakening.
664. **Ye** is properly nominative case, but is used here instead of *you* for the sake of the rhyme.
672. **Not** = not even.
694, etc. "Such a strange and romantic dream as may be naturally expected to flow from the extraordinary events of the past day. It might, perhaps, be quoted as one of Mr. Scott's most successful efforts in descriptive poetry. Some few lines of it are indeed unrivalled for delicacy and melancholy tenderness." — *Critical Review*.
704. **Grisly.** Horrible, frightful.
706. **Affright.** Would now be *fright*.
721. How quiet the night must have been!
727. **Communed.** Notice the accent.
738. **Orisons.** Prayers.
740. **Told.** To *tell* is to count; e.g., "to tell one's beads." Cf. *teller* and *tally*.

CANTO SECOND.

The Island.

1. **Jetty.** Black as jet.
7. **Minstrel.** "Highland chieftains, to a late period, retained in their service the bard, as a family officer." — *Scott*.
19. **High place.** Supply *be* after *place*.
35. Remember what happened to you formerly.
37. **Main.** Principal body of water. Cf. *mainland*.
56. **As** = as if.
74. Was it a breach of fidelity to Malcolm that Ellen showed some interest in the stranger?
80. **Fair.** Cf. i. 449 and 528.
86. **After** should be *afterward* in prose. *After* is properly a preposition or a conjunction, but no longer an adverb.

94. **Parts** = departs. Cf. *dewing*, *wildered*, used for *bedewing* and *bewildered*.

100. **Had** = would have.

106. **Thee** would be *thyself* in prose.

109. "The ancient and powerful family of Graham (which, for metrical reasons, is here spelled after the Scottish pronunciation) held extensive possessions in the counties of Dumbarton and Stirling. Few families can boast of more historical renown, having claim to three of the most remarkable characters in the Scottish annals, Sir John the Græme, the celebrated Marquis of Montrose, and John Græme, of Claverhouse, Viscount of Dundee." — *Scott*.

112. **In hall and bower** = among men and women.

131. **Erst** = formerly. See i. 42. **Saint Modan**. A Scotch abbot of the seventh century. "I am not prepared to show that Saint Modan was a performer on the harp. It was, however, no unsaintly accomplishment." — *Scott*.

141. Bothwell Castle is on the Clyde, near Glasgow.

142. An allusion to the downfall of the Douglases of the house of Angus, during the reign of James V.

143. **Heaven** = sky, and so country.

151. **Fraught**. Filled with. Cf. *Freight*.

159. **From Tweed to Spey** = from one extremity to the other; throughout Scotland. **What marvel.** What wonder is it that, etc.

161. **Confusedly**. See i. 272.

166. **Sire**. The subject of resigned, in 168.

170. **Reave**. Rob, tear away. Now obsolete in prose. Cf. *bereave* and *rive*.

172. **For** = as for.

186. **Wiled**. Coaxed, as by flattery.

194. **Birthright** is here an adjective.

198. **Leading star** = lode-star.

200. **Bleeding Heart** was the badge of the Douglas family.

206. **Strathspey**. A lively Scottish dance, common in the *strath*, or valley, of the River Spey. See l. 159.

209. See 172.

213. **Clan-Alpine's pride.** Clan-Alpine = descendants of Alpin or Alpine, an ancient king of Scotland. Hence Mac Alpine.

214. **Loch Lomond**. About twenty-three miles long and five broad.

216. The Lennox family dwelt south of Loch Lomond, and gave their name to that district.

221. **Holy-Rood.** The royal palace at Edinburgh.

227-231. This is not an exaggeration. **Woe the day** = may woe be to the day.

234. Supply *that* after *now*.

235. **Guerdon.** Reward.

236. **Dispensation.** This was necessary because Roderick and Ellen were cousins.

240. Supply *may* before *be*.

251. **Orphan,** from its position, would seem to be in apposition to *she*, but it is in apposition to *child*.

260. **Maronnan's cell.** At the eastern extremity of Loch Lomond.

270. **Bracklinn's.** For linn see i. 71.

271. **Save** = except when, unless. In prose *save* is not good either as conjunction or as preposition.

275, 276. The sword itself would feel more mercy than would Roderick.

292. **Instinctive.** Adjective for adverb.

303. **Woe the while.** See 227, and i. 166.

306. **Tine-man.** "Archibald, the third Earl of Douglas, was so unfortunate in all his enterprises, that he acquired the epithet of Tineman, because he *tined*, or lost, his followers in every battle which he fought." — *Scott.*

307. **What time** = at the time when. Cf. Latin *quo tempore*.

309, 310. See i. 536, 537.

311. **Harbored** = taken shelter. Rare as an intransitive verb.

319. **Beltane.** A May-day Celtic festival.

327. **Canna.** Cotton-grass.

330. **Pibroch.** See i. 638.

335. **Glengyle.** A valley at the upper end of Loch Katrine.

337. **Brianchoil.** On the north shore of Loch Katrine.

340. **Pine.** The emblem of Clan-Alpine.

343. **Tartans brave.** Gay plaids.

345. **Bonnets.** Here means men's caps.

351. **Chanters.** Pipes of the bagpipes.

357. **Sound.** The first edition has *sounds*.

362. **Gathering.** The tune for summoning the clans to gather together for war.

367. **Hurrying** belongs to the noun for which *their* stands.

392. **Burden.** The subject, theme, chorus, refrain. The "burden" of this song was, "Roderich Vich Alpine dhu, ho! ieroe!" See i. 17.

399. Notice the change from iambic to dactylic metre. The dactyl is a foot of one accented, followed by two unaccented, syllables.

400. **Pine.** See l. 340.

405. **Bourgeon.** Sprout, bud.

408. **Vich** = son, or descendant; **dhu** = black. Black Roderick, the descendant of Alpine.

410. **Beltane.** Here used to denote the season, May. See 319.

412. **The more.** In this phrase *the* is called an adverb.

416. **Menteith.** See i. 89. **Breadalbane.** The country north of Loch Lomond, around Loch Tay, extending as far west as Perthshire.

419. **Glen Fruin.** A valley south-west of Loch Lomond.

420. **Slogan.** The battle-cry of the Highlanders.

421. **Bannochar, Glen Luss,** and **Ross-dhu** are in the neighborhood of Glen Fruin.

426. **Lennox.** See 216. **Leven-glen.** The valley of the Leven, a river which connects Loch Lomond with the Clyde.

431. **The rosebud.** Ellen. O that Ellen should marry Roderick and bear him offspring!

446. **Passion.** In apposition to Ellen. **His.** The Chieftain, her kinsman's.

454. **Mid-path.** Midway, half-way.

465, 466. Some feelings with less of earth in them than heaven are given to mortals. Observe the double, or feminine, rhyme. Accent and rhyme fall on the penult; that is, there is an extra, unaccented syllable at the end. (See Parsons's "English Versification.")

476. **Weep'd.** Used only for the rhyme.

497. **Percy's Norman pennon.** Won by the Earl of Douglas in 1388. It furnished the theme of Scotch and English ballads. Perhaps Ellen's father carried it as a trophy, and perhaps a later capture of a pennon is alluded to.

501. **Pomp.** Triumphal procession.

506. **Blantyre.** A priory opposite Bothwell Castle.

508. **As.** The correlative of *so* in 502.

529. **Aught.** An adverb here, qualifying *o'erweigh'd*.

541. **Ptarmigan.** White grouse.
548. **Ben Lomond.** The highest mountain near Loch Lomond.
549. Notice the peculiar meaning of **sob. Confess.** See i. 377.
571, 572. If I were deprived of that gallant pastime, all that I have left of the characteristics of Douglas would be reft from me.
574. **Glenfinlas** = "glen of the green women."
577. **Royal ward.** Under the guardianship of the king, because without natural guardians and under age.
578. **Risked.** By assisting Douglas, an outlaw.
582. **Spleen.** Anger. For the cause of the *spleen*, see 315-322.
591. **Light** = light-armed.
594. **Were the news.** *News* is singular now.
601. **As.** See 56.
616. In 1529 James swept through Ettrick Forest with an army of ten thousand men, and "tamed the Border-side."
623. **Loud cries their blood.** For vengeance. The *Meggat* flows into the Yarrow, the Yarrow into the Ettrick, the Ettrick into the Tweed. The *Teviot* also flows into the Tweed.
638. Give me your counsel in the difficulties that I disclose.
642. **This.** Ellen. **That.** Margaret.
674. **Allies.** Here accented on the first syllable. **Enow** = enough.
678. **Links.** Windings.
679. **Stirling's porch.** Stirling Castle was a favorite residence of the Scotch kings.
683. **Blench** = shrink.
692. After *are* supply *those.* Cf. Latin *sunt qui.*
702. **Battled.** Battlemented.
708. **Astound.** Shortened from *astounded* for the metre.
726, 727. For similar construction, see i. 407.
747. **Nighted** = benighted. Cf. *wildered, dewing,* etc.
763. **Parting** = departing. See preceding line.
774. See 319.
776. **Punishment delayed** = delay of punishment. See i. 389.
782. **Had been** = would have been.
786. I shall regard as my foe the first who strikes.
798. **As** = as if.
801. Addressed to Malcolm. "Hardihood was in every respect so essential to the character of a Highlander, that the reproach of effeminacy was the most bitter that could be thrown upon him." — *Scott.*

804. **Fell.** Hill.
805. **Lackey.** To attend as a lackey. Not common as a verb.
807. If he would know more, you (spy that you are) can tell him.
809. "This officer is a sort of secretary, and is to be ready, upon all occasions, to venture his life in defence of his master." — *Scott.*
812. **Hold.** See i. 574.
824. **But** = that not.
826. **Said** = finished speaking.
831. **Fiery cross.** "When a chieftain designed to summon his clan upon any sudden or important emergency, he slew a goat, and making a cross of any light wood, seared its extremities in the fire, and extinguished them in the blood of the animal. This was called the *Fiery Cross*, also *Crean Tarigh*, or the Cross of Shame, because disobedience to what the symbol implied inferred infamy. It was delivered to a swift and trusty messenger, who ran full speed with it to the next hamlet, where he presented it to the principal person, with a single word, implying the place of rendezvous. He who received the symbol was bound to send it forward, with equal despatch, to the next village; and thus it passed with incredible celerity through all the district which owed allegiance to the chief, and also among his allies and neighbors, if the danger was common to them. At sight of the Fiery Cross every man, from sixteen years old to sixty, capable of bearing arms, was obliged instantly to repair, in his best arms and accoutrements, to the place of rendezvous. He who failed to appear suffered the extremities of fire and sword, which were emblematically denounced to the disobedient by the bloody and burnt marks upon this warlike signal." — *Scott.*
835. It would be safest to land far up the lake.
836. **Himself** = he himself; i.e., Allan.
839. **Roll'd** goes with *plaid*, next line.
843. **Abrupt.** Adjective for adverb.
846. **Point** = point out.
847. **Ward.** See 577.
855. Observe the sudden **break** in the sentence.

CANTO THIRD.

The Gathering.

1. **Yore** = of years; of old.
3. **Legends store.** See i. 548.
4. **Ventures** = adventures.
7. **Wait** = await.
8. **Tide** is the object of *wait*.
10. For omission see ii. 692.
15. See ii. 307; and also i. 319, 500.
16. **Kindred banner** = banner of their kindred, or clan.
17. **Gathering sound** = sound, or signal, for gathering.
18. **Fiery Cross.** See ii. 831.
19. See Ruskin's "Modern Painters," vol. iii. 278.
39. **Cushat dove.** Ring dove.
46. **Impatient blade.** See i. 122.
50. For antiquity (men of old) had taught that such ritual was a fitting preface.
62. **Rowan.** The mountain ash.
63. **Shivers.** Cf. v. 569.
67. **Grizzled.** Sometimes spelt *grisled*. Slightly gray.
71. **Monk** is the object of *had drawn*.

"The state of religion in the Middle Ages afforded considerable facilities for those whose mode of life excluded them from regular worship, to secure, nevertheless, the ghostly assistance of confessors, perfectly willing to adapt the nature of their doctrine to the necessities and peculiar circumstances of their flock." — *Scott*.

74. **Benharrow.** A mountain near Loch Lomond.
76. **Druid's.** The Druids were priests in Britain.
80. **Mix'd** = was mixed.
81. **Hallow'd creed.** Christianity as contrasted with *heathen lore*.
85. **Bound** = boundary.
87. **Strath.** Broader valley than *glen*.
88. **Desert-dweller.** Same as *Hermit*. **His.** The huntsman's.
89. **He.** The huntsman. **Between;** i.e., between his prayers.
91. **Brian's birth.** This story is based on a local legend.

102. That served as buckler to a heart unknown to fear, or to which fear was unknown.

104. **Fieldfare.** A kind of thrush.

108. **Full** = full blown.

114, 116. **Snood.** "The *snood*, or riband with which a Scottish lass braided her hair, had an emblematical signification, and applied to her maiden character. It was exchanged for the *curch*, *toy*, or *coif*, when she passed, by marriage, into the matron state. But if the damsel was so unfortunate as to lose pretensions to the name of maiden, without gaining a right to that of matron, she was neither permitted to use the snood, nor advanced to the graver dignity of the curch." — *Scott.* See i. 363.

120. In prose we should have *either . . . or.*

130. **Hap.** Lot, fate. Cf. *happen, haply, perhaps.* **To wail** = in wailing.

136. **Cloister.** Literally an enclosed place; hence, monastery. Personification. **Pitying gate.** See 46, and i. 122.

138. **Sable-letter'd.** Old English type is sometimes called "black letter."

142. **Cabala.** Mysteries.

149. "In adopting the legend concerning the birth of the founder of the church of Kilmalie, the author has endeavored to trace the effects which such a belief was likely to produce, in a barbarous age, on the person to whom it related." — *Scott.*

154. **River Demon.** "The River Demon, or River-horse, for it is that form which he commonly assumes, is the Kelpy of the Lowlands, an evil and malicious spirit, delighting to forebode and to witness calamity. He frequents most Highland lakes and rivers; and one of his most memorable exploits was performed upon the banks of Loch Vennachar, in the very district which forms the scene of our action. It consisted in the destruction of a funeral procession, with all its attendants." — *Scott.*

156. **Noontide hag or goblin grim.** "The 'noontide hag,' called in Gaelic *Glas-lich*, a tall, emaciated, gigantic female figure, is supposed in particular to haunt the district of Knoidart. A goblin dressed in antique armor, and having one hand covered with blood, called, from that circumstance, *Lham-dearg*, or Red-hand, is a tenant of the forests of Glenmore and Rothiemurcus." — *Scott.*

161. **Mankind.** Notice the unusual accent.

NOTES ON THE LADY OF THE LAKE. 233

168. **Ben-Shie.** "Woman of the fairies."
"Most great families in the Highlands were supposed to have a tutelar, or rather a domestic, spirit, attached to them, who took an interest in their prosperity, and intimated, by its wailings, any approaching disaster. . . . The Ben-Shie implies the female fairy whose lamentations were often supposed to precede the death of a chieftain of particular families. When she is visible, it is in the form of an old woman, with a blue mantle and streaming hair." — *Scott.*

171. **Shingly.** Gravelly.

177. **Ban.** Curse.

189. **A cubit's length** = 18 inches.

191. **Inch-Cailliach.** "Isle of Nuns," or of "Old Women," at the lower extremity of Loch Lomond.

194. "The burial-ground continues to be used, and contains the family places of sepulture of several neighboring clans." — *Scott.*

198. **Anathema.** Curse.

203. **Dwelling low.** Grave.

208. **Him** is the indirect object. "Shall doom him to wrath and woe," would be the common construction.

212. **Strook** = struck; used for the rhyme.

214–217. Notice the repetition of rhyme.

237. **Volumed** = voluminous.

243. **Goshawk** = goose-hawk.

247. **Answering** goes with **cry**, 242.

253. **Coir-Uriskin.** "This is a very steep and most romantic hollow in the mountain of Benvenue, overhanging the southeastern extremity of Loch Katrine. . . . A dale in so wild a situation, and amid a people whose genius bordered on the romantic, did not remain without appropriate deities. The name literally implies the Corri, or Den, of the Wild or Shaggy Men. . . . Tradition has ascribed to the *Urisk*, who gives name to the cavern, a figure between a goat and a man; in short, however much the classical reader may be startled, precisely that of the Grecian satyr. . . . It must be owned that the *Coir*, or Den, does not, in its present state, meet our ideas of a subterraneous grotto or cave, being only a small and narrow cavity among huge fragments of rocks rudely piled together. But such a scene is liable to convulsions of nature which a Lowlander cannot estimate, and which may have choked up what was originally a cavern. At least the name and tradition warrant the author of a ficti-

tious tale to assert its having been such at the remote period in which this scene is laid." — *Scott.*

255. **Beala-nam-bo.** "The pass of the cattle."

261. **The** = that.

263. **Saw and disobey'd** = should see and disobey.

265. **Among.** Misused for *in*.

275. Observe the pronunciation of **hearth** for the rhyme.

278, 279. May the blessing (pardon, or salvation) that is bought for all others by this sign be denied to him.

285. **Henchman.** See ii. 809.

286. **Lanrick mead.** A meadow near Loch Vennachar.

297. **Wide** = distant.

299. **Blood and brand.** Cf. the more common *fire and sword*.

300. **Deer's hide.** The Highlanders wore brogues, or brogans, made of half-dried leather. **Dun** = dark brown.

309. **Questing.** Seeking, hunting.

310. **Scaur.** A steep cliff.

320. **Warrior.** Here an adjective.

327. **Place.** See 286.

332. **Cheer.** Face, look, countenance.

337. **At bay.** See i. 133.

344. **Bosky.** Woody, bushy.

346. Supply *that* at the beginning of the line.

349. **Duncraggan.** Between Loch Achray and Loch Vennachar, near the Brigg of Turk.

352. **Thou.** Malise. The lord of Duncraggan's huts now takes the Fiery Cross.

355. **Him** = himself, as frequently before.

369. **Coronach.** "A wild expression of lamentation poured forth by the mourners over the body of a departed friend;" a funeral song.

370. The metre is irregular; the prevailing foot seems to be the amphibrach, three syllables, the second being accented. Some of the lines have an unnecessary foot at the beginning.

384. **Flushing** = full bloom.

386. **Correi.** "The hollow side of a hill, where game usually lies;" hence, "fleet in pursuit of game."

387. **Cumber.** Vexation, embarrassment, perplexity.

388. **Red;** i.e., with blood; hence, bold, daring.

394. **Stumah.** A dog; "Faithful."

403. **Urge.** We should expect *urges* in prose. *Urge* is ungrammatical.

433. **That** has for its antecedent *his*, in the preceding line.

434. **The oak.** Duncan. **The sapling bough.** Angus.

436. **His duty done.** The absolute construction here has the force of a condition.

439. **Hest** = behest. Cf. *wildered, dewing*, etc.

440. **To arms.** Notice the omission of the verb from this imperative exclamation.

445. **Targe.** See i. 546, and v. 380.

447. **Mourner's.** The widow's.

450. **Borrow'd force.** The energy borrowed from, or caused by, the "weapon-clang and martial call."

452. Trace on the map the progress of the signal through the small district of lakes and mountains: first to Duncraggan, thence towards Callander, up the pass of Leny, to the Chapel of Saint Bride, at Strath-Ire, along Loch Lubnaig, through the districts of Balquidder, Glenfinlas, and Strath-Gartney.

453. **Strath-Ire.** The valley between Loch Voil and Loch Lubnaig.

458. **Teith's young waters.** The branches of the Teith, especially the Leny, on the bank of which stood the Chapel of Saint Bride.

461. See 458. **Saint Bride,** or Saint Bridget, was an Irish nun of the fifth century.

465. **Sympathetic;** i.e., in sympathy with the dancing waves, dizzy.

472, 473. Instead of the fully expressed conclusion, we have the exclamation. If he had fallen there, we should have had to say farewell forever to Duncraggan's orphan heir.

475. **Firmer.** Should be *more firmly* in prose.

478. **Rout.** See i. 67.

480, 481. **Tombea, Armandave.** Places in the neighborhood of Strath-Ire.

483. **Bridal,** here a noun, = wedding-party.

485. **Coif-clad.** See 114.

487. **Snooded.** See 114.

488. **Unwitting.** See i. 596.

489. **Shrilly.** Cf. **steepy,** 304.

495. **Kerchief's.** Cf. **curch,** 114.
517. **O fatal doom!** See 268–279.
526. **Sped him.** *Speed* is usually intransitive; but see 409, 509. For *him* see 355, and elsewhere.
528. The River Leny runs from Loch Lubnaig into the Teith.
529. **Racer's.** Norman's.
530. "Hope deferred maketh the heart sick." — Prov. xiii. 12.
537, 538. For the kind of rhyme, see ii. 465, 466.
541. **Brae.** Hillside, slope, brow.
546. **Bracken.** Fern.
549. **Stilly.** See 346. **Laid** has no noun to limit, but belongs to the noun represented by *my* in the next line. See 433.
561. A time will come when I can allow my heart to be filled with those feelings which now I must suppress.
565. If I shall have returned.
570. **Balquidder.** Near the east end of Loch Voil, and famous as Rob Roy's burial-place. **Blaze** of the heath on the moorlands.
575. **Nor faster than. Nor so far** as.
576. **Voice of war.** Fiery Cross, the signal for war.
577. **Coil.** Confusion, tumult.
583. Each man that could claim. Cf. i. 528.
604. **Menteith.** See i. 89.
607, 608, 609. **Rednock, Cardross,** and **Duchray** were castles in the valley of the Forth.
611. **Wot.** See i. 596.
613, 614. The tenses do not correspond. The metre requires *repair* instead of *repaired*.
617, 618. See ii. 649–664.
622. **Coir-nan-Uriskin.** See 253.
625. A retreat *as* wild and strange. See i. 202.
641. **Still** = stillness.
656. **Satyrs.** See 253.
664. **Beal-nam-bo.** See 255.
671. It was an unusual sight to see the chief *behind* his **men.**
697. **Prove.** Experience, try.
705. **Inly.** We should expect *inwardly* in prose.
713. Notice the peculiar rhyme of this hymn.
729. **Stainless styled** = called pure.
748. **Hastier.** Cf. **firmer,** 475.

CANTO FOURTH.

The Prophecy.

9. **What time.** See ii. 307.
10. **Fond conceit.** Idle or foolish conception.
19. **Bræs of Doune.** The hills near Doune, a town on the Teith.
23. **Scout** = scouting expedition.
36. **Boune.** Ready, prepared.
42. **Bide.** Endure. **Bout.** Turn.
54. **Dear pledge.** See 48 and 49.
55. **Advised.** Planned, considered.
63. **The Taghairm.** "The Highlanders, like all rude people, had various superstitious modes of inquiring into futurity. One of the most noted was the *Taghairm*, mentioned in the text. A person was wrapped up in the skin of a newly-slain bullock, and deposited beside a waterfall, or at the bottom of a precipice, or in some other strange, wild, and unusual situation, where the scenery around him suggested nothing but objects of horror. In this situation, he revolved in his mind the question proposed; and whatever was impressed upon him by his exalted imagination, passed for the inspiration of the disembodied spirits, who haunt these desolate recesses." — *Scott*.
68. **Gallangad.** In the Loch Lomond district.
73. **Kernes.** Light-armed soldiers.
74. **Bealmaha.** "The pass of the plain," east of Loch Lomond.
77. **Dennan's Row.** At the foot of Ben Lomond.
78. **Scatheless.** Harmless.
82. **Boss.** Knob.
83. **Verge.** Pronounced so as to rhyme with *Targe*.
84. **Hero's Targe.** A rock in the forest of Glenfinlas.
98. **Broke.** Quartered.
99. **Morsel.** "There is a little gristle upon the spoone of the brisket, which we call the raven's bone."
115. **Rouse** = rise.
124. **Save he** would be *except him* in prose.
130. **Blazed** = emblazoned.
132, 133. "Though this be in the text described as a response of the Taghairm, or Oracle of the Hide, it was of itself an augury fre-

quently attended to. The fate of the battle was often anticipated, in the imagination of the combatants, by observing which party first shed blood." — *Scott.*

Notice how this prophecy is quoted in v. 331, 332.

150. **Glaive.** Sword.
174. **Stance.** Station.
182. **I.** Scott.
199. **They.** The boats, 195.
223. **Trow'd.** Thought, believed.
227. Both Malcolm and Roderick are in danger on our account.
230. See ii. 823, 824.
231. **Cambus-Kenneth's fane.** An abbey on the Forth, near Stirling.
236. **Had** = would have.
237. If I had been his son instead of his daughter.
244. See 220.
245. **Bode.** Foretell.
250, 251. My prophecy of fear was true, therefore believe my prophecy of cheer.
253. **Still** = always.
261. "This little fairy tale is founded upon a very curious Danish ballad which occurs in a collection of heroic songs first published in 1591." — *Scott.*

Observe peculiarities in the metre and the rhyme.

262. **Mavis.** Thrush. **Merle.** Blackbird.
267. **Wold.** Open country.
268. **Wont.** See i. 408.
277. **Pall.** Purple cloth used for making palls, or mantles.
283. **Darkling** = in the dark.
285. **Vair.** Fur.
291. **Richard.** Notice the peculiar accent.
298. **Won'd.** Dwelt.
302. **Screen** is in apposition to *beech* and *oak.*
330. **Kindly blood** = blood of kinsman.
340. The "demon elf" speaks now.
357. **Wist I** = if I knew.
363, 364. **The.** See ii. 412.
371. **Dunfermline gray.** The old abbey in Dunfermline, near Edinburgh.

NOTES ON THE LADY OF THE LAKE.

377. **Claims.** The rhyme requires the singular form; perhaps the subjects are taken singly.
387. **Bourne.** Limit, boundary.
392. Observe the omission. **Scathe.** Harm. See 78
402. **Worthy** is followed by *of* in prose.
411. **Bochastle.** For different accent see i. 106.
413. **Bower.** Dwelling. See i. 217.
417. **Before;** i.e., when he visited the Island.
419. **That fatal bait.** The knowledge that my selfish ear was soothed to hear my praise.
421. **Atone** is here a transitive verb = atone for.
425. **Thou** means herself.
437. **Train.** Device, snare.
446. Notice the ellipsis.
455. **If** = whether.
459. Cf. 446.
471. **Lordship.** Land held by a lord.
473. I who reck of (care for) neither state nor land.
484. **Wending.** Going.
495. See i. 155-167.
500. **Fared.** Went. Cf. *Farewell, wayfarer, thoroughfare.*
506. **Weeds.** Garments.
531, 532. These two streams join the Forth near Stirling.
552. **Bridegroom.** Notice the unusual accent.
555. **Maudlin.** A corruption of Magdalene.
565. **To break his fall.** When he is pitched from the cliff, l. 558.
567. **Batten.** Fatten.
590-603. Blanche warns Fitz-James of the ambush that was set for him.
590. **Toils.** Nets.
594. Fitz-James is the "stag." **Ten.** Ten branches on his antlers.
598. **Wounded doe;** i.e., Blanche.
617. **Thrill'd.** Quivered.
635. **Slower.** See iii. 475, 748.
642. **Daggled.** Moistened, wet.
672. **Wreak.** Avenge.
734, 735. Notice the omissions of verbs. There is no time for words that may be easily supplied.

744. **The privilege of chase** is mentioned in the next two lines.
746. **Slip.** Set loose.
749. Notice the abrupt break in the sentence.
754. **I write** = and I will write.
761. **Cheer.** Fare, entertainment. Cf. i. 442, and iii. 332.
772. **A mighty augury.** The Taghairm. See 63.
788. **Warrant.** Security.
794. **Wreath;** i.e., the "gathered heath."

CANTO FIFTH.

The Combat.

17. Their soldier meal was as short and rude as their matins.
18. "The Scottish Highlander calls himself *Gael*, or Gaul, and terms the Lowlanders, *Sassenach*, or Saxons." — *Scott.*
22. **Winded.** See i. 319.
46. **Shingles.** Gravel. Cf. **Shingly,** iii. 171.
51. **Dank.** Moist, damp.
60. **Traversed.** Notice the unusual accent.
64. **Sooth to tell** = to tell the truth. Cf. i. 476; iv. 250.
78. It is enough to say that I sought, etc.
92. **But** = that.
102. **Show** yourself to be.
108. See 124.
124. The Duke of Albany, son of a younger brother of James III., was regent of Scotland after the death of James IV.
"There is scarcely a more disorderly period of Scottish history than that which succeeded the battle of Flodden, and occupied the minority of James V. Feuds of ancient standing broke out like old wounds; and every quarrel among the independent nobility, which occurred daily, and almost hourly, gave rise to fresh bloodshed." — *Scott.*
126. **Mew'd.** Shut up.
132. **Methinks** = it seems to me.
145. **Reft.** Robbed.
148. **Ask we;** i.e., if we ask.
161. **Rears** = raises. **Shock** = sheaf.
186. For ellipsis, see 78. **Promise.** See iv. 685–688.

196–227. This incident is founded on fact. The most dramatic situation in the poem.

252. **Glinted.** Flashed.

268. Though every valley, etc., depended on our strife.

298. Katrine, Achray, and Vennachar.

309. **This murderous chief,** as you call me. See 105, 106.

326. **Means.** "'Means,' in the sense of instrument — e.g., 'a means to an end,' 'this was the sole means within reach' — is usually, though perhaps not always, treated as singular; but in the sense of income, — e.g., 'his means are ample' — it is plural." — "*Hill's Foundations of Rhetoric,*" p. 45.

331, 332. Cf. iv. 132, 133.

336. See iv. 618–632.

344. **Strengths** = strongholds.

350. As to name homage.

362. See iv. 679, 680.

364. **Ruth.** Pity.

371. See 262, 263.

380. **Targe.** "A round target of light wood, covered with strong leather and studded with brass or iron, was a necessary part of a Highlander's equipment. . . . A person thus armed had a considerable advantage in private fray." — *Scott.*

See i. 546; iii. 445.

383. **Train'd abroad.** See i. 163.

401. **Borne** belongs to *Chieftain* in the next line.

442. See iv. 548–674.

465. **Weed.** See iv. 506.

496. **Glance** and **disappear** are infinitives.

550. James II. stabbed William, eighth Earl of Douglas, at Stirling Castle.

551. **O sad and fatal mound!** State criminals were executed on an eminence at the northeast of the Castle.

562. **Morrice-dancers.** For a description of the game, etc., see Scott's "Abbot," ch. xiv., and "The Fair Maid of Perth," ch. xvi. and note on ch. xx.

569. **Shivers.** See iii. 63.

584. **Jennet.** A small Spanish horse.

586. Who smiled for pride, and blushed for shame (bashfulness), at being noticed by the king.

614. **Robin Hood:** "The exhibition of this renowned outlaw and his band was a favorite frolic at such festivals." — *Scott.*
See Scott's "Abbot," note G to ch. xiv.
626. **Stake.** Prize.
630. **Wight.** Valiant. Sometimes a noun meaning *person.*
638. **Fare.** Fate.
641. "The usual prize of a wrestling was a ram and a ring, but the animal would have embarrassed my story." — *Scott.*
653. **Rood** = rod.
660. **Ladies' Rock.** "A small rocky mount, in the valley, on the Castle-hill, where the fair ones of the court took their station to behold these feats."
666. **And** (with) **sharper glance.**
697. **Archery** = archers.
724. **Needs** = it needs; only a blow is needed.
728. In the first edition this line reads, "Clamoured his comrades of the train."
740. **Misproud** = wrongfully proud.
752. **Misarray** = disorder.
768. **Hyndford.** On the Clyde.
790. Notice the anticipation, "prolepsis."
796. **Amain.** The first edition has *again.*
809. **Some bier** (of a) **beloved** (friend).
819. **Changeling** = changeful.
829. All these adjectives belong to **herd,** in the preceding line.
838. **Cognizance.** Badge.
856. **Lost** (sight of) **it.** Forgot it.
866. **Leaders lost** = loss of their leaders. Cf. i. 388 and ii. 776.
868, 869. I do not wish to have the common people feel avenging steel on account of their Chief's crimes.
887. See 550.

CANTO SIXTH.

The Guard-Room.

3. **Caitiff.** Strictly a *captive;* hence a wretched man.
15. **Gyve.** Fetter. Commonly used in the plural, *gyves.*
63. **Holytide** = holy time, holiday.
87. **Catch.** Song; usually a part-song.

NOTES ON THE LADY OF THE LAKE.

88. **Buxom.** Literally bow-some; i.e. bending; hence yielding, obedient; then lively.

90. **Poule** = Paul. The prevailing foot of the song is the anapest, — two unaccented, followed by an accented, syllable.

92. **Black-jack.** A leather pitcher.

93. **Seven deadly sins.** Pride, idleness, gluttony, lust, avarice, envy, wrath.

95. **Upsees.** "Bacchanalian interjection borrowed from the Dutch." — *Scott*.

100. **Gillian.** A corruption of Juliana. The shorter form is Gill, or Jill.

103. **Cure.** Office of Parish priest. **Placket and pot.** Women and wine.

104. **Lurch.** Swindle, cheat.

124. **Store.** See i. 548; iii. 3.

136. Mar bade that I should provide steed for them.

144. **Fee.** A kiss.

167. **I shame me** = I am ashamed.

170. **Needwood.** A forest in Staffordshire.

183. **Tullibardine.** In Perthshire, where the Murrays lived.

208. The King's pledge of claims on his gratitude.

221. **Hest** = behest, command.

222. Permit that I marshal you; more commonly, permit me to, etc.

234. **Barret-cap.** Flat cap.

265. **But.** If not.

292, 293. 295-299. These lines are not in the first edition.

295. **Leech.** Physician.

305. They deemed that he sought the chief, Roderick. See 242 and 269.

306. **Prore** = prow.

347. **Dermid's race.** The Campbells.

369. **Beal' an Duine.** "The pass of the man."

"A skirmish actually took place at a pass thus called in the Trosachs, and closed with the remarkable incident mentioned in the text. It was greatly posterior in date to the reign of James V." — *Scott*.

377. **Eyrie.** Nest of a bird of prey. Other spellings are *eyry aery*, *aerie*. **Erne.** Eagle.

405. **Battalia** = battalion.
414. **Vaward** = vanguard.
452. **Tinchel.** " A circle of sportsmen, who, by surrounding a great space, and gradually narrowing, brought immense quantities of deer together, which usually made desperate efforts to break through the *Tinchel*." — *Scott*.
487. **Bracklinn.** "This is a beautiful cascade made by a mountain stream called the Keltie, at a place called the Bridge of Bracklinn, about a mile from the village of Callander, in Menteith." — *Scott*.
488. **Linn.** See preceding line; also i. 71, and ii. 270.
539. **Bonnet-pieces.** Gold coins stamped with the king's head, with a bonnet on it. **Store.** See 124. " I will give my purse to him who will swim," etc.
545. **Casque.** Helmet. **Corselet.** Armor to protect the front of the body.
610. **Breadalbane.** See ii. 416.
638. **Storied.** Cf. Gray's " Elegy," *Storied urn*, and Milton's " Il Penseroso," *Storied windows*.
668. **Thrall** = thraldom.
707. **Prime.** First, first part of, early.
712. **Stayed.** Steadied, supported.
720. **Even** = evening.
726. **Presence** = presence-chamber, room of state.
737. **Sheen.** See i. 208.
740. "This discovery will probably remind the reader of the beautiful Arabian tale of 'Il Bondocani.' Yet the incident is not borrowed from that elegant story, but from Scottish tradition." — *Scott*.
741-744. "When used for the former purpose [to impress a thought] exclusively, the illustration should as a rule come first, that it may, by calling up appropriate ideas, prepare the mind for what is to follow. If, in such a case, it came second, it would serve no purpose but that of ornament, and it might seriously interrupt the flow of thought. Hence the propriety of the order adopted in the following lines : —

> ' *As wreath of snow*, on mountain breast,
> Slides from the rock that gave it rest,
> *Poor Ellen glided* from her stay,
> And at the monarch's feet she lay.'

"Evidently the first two lines are not needed to render the third line intelligible. As they stand, they create sympathy with Ellen; if placed after the third line, they would obstruct the narrative; for, the moment the reader knows that Ellen is at the King's feet, his interest in the manner of her getting there is lost in his desire to know what happened next." — *A. S. Hill's* "*Principles of Rhetoric,*" pp. 148, 149.

779, 780. Yet James did not wish that the crowd should long look curiously on the natural raptures [felt by a daughter at her father's safety].

782. **Proselyte** is in keeping with *infidel* and *misbeliever* (implied in *misbelieving* and *doubting*) in the preceding stanza.

784. **Speed.** Success.

802. **Talisman.** Spell, or magic charm. See iv. 464.

813. **Grace:** Pardon.

842. See beginning of poem.

846. Lending to the fountain and the wild breeze thy wilder minstrelsy.

849. **Fold and lea.** Sheepfold and meadow.

850. **Housing.** Returning to the house, or hive.

ENGLISH LITERATURE.

Of our popular list of classics the editor of the Christian Union recently said: "*We cannot speak too highly of the Students' Series of English Classics.*" There are nearly thirty books now out and in preparation, and it is only necessary to read the list of our editors to gain an intelligent idea of the character of the work done. We do not add to this series for the sake of increasing the list, but we shall make the same careful selection of authors that are to come as we have in those announced. Any book announced in this series will be worth the attention of an instructor in English Literature.

Painter's Introduction to English Literature, including several Classical Works. With Notes.

By Professor F. V. N. PAINTER, of Roanoke College, Va. Cloth. Pages xviii+628. Introduction and mailing price, **$1.25.**

Morgan's English and American Literature.

By HORACE H. MORGAN, LL.D., formerly of St. Louis High School. A practical working text-book for schools and colleges. Pages viii+261. Introduction price, **$1.00.**

Introduction to the Study of English Literature.

In Six Lectures. By Professor GEORGE C. S. SOUTHWORTH. Cloth. Pages 194. Introduction price, **75 cents.**

The Students' Series of English Classics.

PRICES REDUCED. To furnish the educational public with well-edited editions of those authors used in, or required for admission to, many of the colleges, the Publishers announce this new series. *The following books are now ready,* and others are in preparation. *They are uniformly bound in cloth,* furnished at a *comparatively low price,* and Students of Literature should buy such texts that after use in the class room will be found valuable for the library.

LITERATURE.

Coleridge's Ancient Mariner	**25 cents.**
A Ballad Book	50 ,,
The Merchant of Venice	35 ,,
Edited by KATHARINE LEE BATES, Wellesley College.	
Matthew Arnold's Sohrab and Rustum	25 ,,
Webster's First Bunker Hill Oration	25 ,,
Milton's L'Allegro, Il Penseroso, Comus, and Lycidas . . .	25 ,,
Edited by LOUISE MANNING HODGKINS, formerly Professor of English Literature, Wellesley College.	
Introduction to the Writings of John Ruskin	50 ,,
Macaulay's Essay on Lord Clive	35 ,,
Edited by VIDA D. SCUDDER, Wellesley College.	
George Eliot's Silas Marner	35 ,,
Scott's Marmion	35 ,,
Edited by MARY HARRIOTT NORRIS, Professor, New York.	
Sir Roger de Coverley Papers from The Spectator	35 ,,
Edited by A. S. ROE, Worcester, Mass.	
Macaulay's Second Essay on the Earl of Chatham	35 ,,
Edited by W. W. CURTIS, High School, Pawtucket, R. I.	
Johnson's History of Rasselas	35 ,,
Edited by FRED N. SCOTT, University of Michigan.	
Macaulay's Essays on Milton and Addison	35 ,,
Edited by JAMES CHALMERS, Professor of Literature.	
Carlyle's Diamond Necklace	35 ,,
Edited by W. A. MOZIER, High School, Ottawa, Ill.	
Joan of Arc, and other selections from De Quincey . . .	35 ,,
Edited by HENRY H. BELFIELD, Chicago Manual Training School.	
Selections from Washington Irving	50 ,,
Edited by ISAAC THOMAS, High School, New Haven, Conn.	
Goldsmith's Traveller and Deserted Village	25 ,,
Edited by W. F. GREGORY, High School, Hartford, Conn.	
Burke's Speech on Conciliation with America	35 ,,
Edited by L. DUPONT SYLE, University of California.	

LITERATURE.

Tennyson's Elaine . . . . **25 cents.**
    Edited by FANNIE MORE MCCAULEY, Instructor, Winchester School, Baltimore.

Macaulay's Life of Samuel Johnson . . . . **25** ,,
    Edited by GAMALIEL BRADFORD, Jr., Instructor in English Literature, Wellesley and Boston.

Scott's Lady of the Lake . . . . **35** ,,
    Edited by JAMES ARTHUR TUFTS, Phillips Exeter Academy.

The following volumes are in preparation:

GOLDSMITH'S VICAR OF WAKEFIELD. Edited by J. G. RIGGS, School Superintendent, Plattsburg, N. Y.

MILTON'S PARADISE LOST, BOOKS I AND II. Edited by ALBERT S. COOK, Yale University.

DE QUINCEY'S THE FLIGHT OF A TARTAR TRIBE. Edited by FRANK T. BAKER, Teachers' College, New York City.

CARLYLE'S ESSAY ON BURNS. Edited by WILLIAM K. WICKES, High School, Syracuse, New York.

TENNYSON'S THE PRINCESS. Edited by HENRY W. BOYNTON, Phillips Academy, Andover, Mass.

LAYS OF ANCIENT ROME. Edited by D. D. PRATT, High School, Portsmouth, Ohio.

WORDSWORTH'S WHITE DOE OF RYLSTONE. Edited by MARY HARRIOTT NORRIS, Professor of English Literature.

We cannot speak too highly of the STUDENTS' SERIES OF ENGLISH CLASSICS. — *The Christian Union.*

Correspondence invited.

LEACH, SHEWELL, & SANBORN,
BOSTON.   **NEW YORK.**   **CHICAGO.**

www.ingramcontent.com/pod-product-compliance
Lightning Source LLC
Chambersburg PA
CBHW021353230426
43666CB00006B/504